GOOD NEWS IN ROMANS

Joseph Rhymer graduated in Philosophy from Leeds University
in 1952. For the next eleven years he was a member of the
Community of the Resurrection; during this time he spent
five years in Barbados as Vice-Principal of Codrington
College. He entered the Roman Catholic Church in 1963.
Since 1968 he has been Senior Lecturer in the Theology
Department of Notre Dame College of Education, Liverpool.
Mr Rhymer has written and edited a number of books on the
Bible, and edits a national educational journal. He is deeply
involved in international and inter-Church co-operation for
teaching about the Bible.

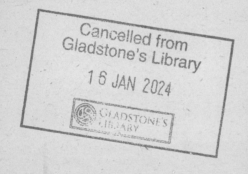

in the same series

GOOD NEWS IN ACTS introduced by David Edwards
GOOD NEWS IN JOHN introduced by Douglas Webster
GOOD NEWS IN LUKE introduced by Wilf Wilkinson

to be published shortly

GOOD NEWS IN GALATIANS introduced by John Davies
GOOD NEWS IN HEBREWS introduced by Thomas Corbishley
GOOD NEWS IN MARK introduced by Robert Crotly

GOOD NEWS IN
ROMANS

Romans in
Today's English Version

Indroduced by
JOSEPH RHYMER

with an Appendix by
Joseph Griffiths

Collins
FONTANA BOOKS
in co-operation with The Bible Reading Fellowship

First published in Fontana Books 1974
© Joseph Rhymer 1974

Today's English Version of *Romans*
© American Bible Society, New York, 1966, 1971

Made and printed in Great Britain by
William Collins Sons & Co Ltd Glasgow

CONTENTS

The Author 9

The Readers 14

The Letter 18

Section 1: 26
Opening Remarks 1:1-17

Section 2: 33
Universal Guilt and Need 1:18-3:20

Section 3: 45
God's Act of Salvation 3:21-5:11

Section 4: 55
God's Power Overcomes Human Weakness
5:12-8:39

Section 5: 77
God's Plan: Jews and Gentiles 9:1-11:36

Section 6: 98
Practical Advice for Life in Christ 12:1-15:13

Section 7: 113
Plans, Greetings and Conclusion 15:14-16:27

Appendix 125
Paul's Letter to the Romans:
An Approach through Literature
   by Joseph Griffiths

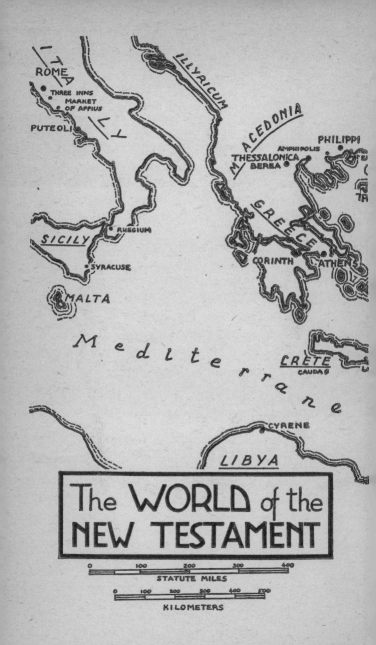

The WORLD of the NEW TESTAMENT

THE AUTHOR

Romans is a letter, a personal message from an intelligent, sensitive and very experienced man to a group of people which included many of his friends. It is also one of the most penetrating and important documents we have about the Christian way of life. But that is by the way. First and foremost it is a letter in which Paul spells out for his readers the Christian faith as he understands it. All through it, the words open windows into the experiences and personality of the remarkable man who wrote it. They show what Jesus Christ means to someone who has staked his whole life on the truth of the gospel.

Not that there were any gospels as we now know them. Mark's gospel, the first of the four gospels, was not written until six or seven years after Paul's letter to the Christians in Rome. This letter tells us what Christians believed during the years before the gospels were written. Already nearly thirty years had passed since the crucifixion and resurrection of Jesus Christ, time for the first generation of Christians to test the truth and the power of Christ's love for themselves. A letter such as this sums up long years of experience, the experience of a very remarkable man and of many other Christians.

By any standards, ancient or modern, Paul stands out as someone who stamps his personality on the people of his time. He would have been thoroughly at home in the modern world of jet travel and international crisis, for his background and his responsibilities made him familiar with the cosmopolitan and sophisticated life of the Romans and the Greeks.

He was a Jew, of course, born into the strictest form of the Jewish religion. Like modern Christianity, there were many forms of the Jewish faith in Paul's time, some very strict and exclusive in their way of life, and some very open and tolerant. Paul belonged to the Pharisee sect, which had been founded during the successful war to free the Jews from Greek rule, a hundred and fifty years before Paul was born. The Pharisees reacted fiercely against all foreign influences on the Jewish religion, and lived by a rigid observance of the Law of Moses in all its detail.

Later, Paul looked back on this period of his life with dismay, but it taught him a lot about religious fanaticism and the effects it can have on people. His letter to the Romans looks closely at the mistakes which people can make when they turn their religion into a legalism. For Paul, Jesus Christ brought a vision of freedom into his life which released him from the fears and restrictions of a religion based on law. It was like leaving school and growing up. In Christianity he found a religion which expected people to think for themselves.

Paul spent the last years of his education in Jerusalem, studying to be a lawyer under one of the most famous Jewish lawyers of the time. Perhaps it was there that he embraced the strictest form of Judaism with all the enthusiasm of a dedicated student.

Most Jews in New Testament times lived outside Palestine, in towns and cities scattered throughout the civilized world. In fact, for more than five hundred years, from the time of the Exile in Babylon, far more Jews had settled outside the Holy Land than within it. With their strong sense of family, and their loyalty to their religion, they were conscious of bonds uniting them together as a people wherever they lived. If they could afford it, they made the pilgrimage to Jerusalem and the magnificent Temple which was the central focus of their religion, but this would be the journey of a lifetime, even for those who could spare time and money for it. Paul was born in Tarsus, a Greek-speaking city in the southern part of Asia Minor.

The widely scattered groups of Jews each had a synagogue in the towns where they lived, but even the strictest of them would be in close contact with the way of life and the thoughts of their non-Jewish neighbours. Paul's Tarsus was a university city and an important port. It commanded the main southern route into the interior of Asia Minor, then one of the richest of all the provinces of the Roman Empire. It would be like living in Bristol or Boston nowadays; no matter how protected a childhood you had, you would catch something of the feel of such an exciting place.

In later life, Paul showed how sympathetic and adaptable he could be with many different kinds of people. Perhaps his childhood in a busy, cosmopolitan city left him with an open-mindedness which could break through the narrow bounds of his religious upbringing. Certainly it helped him when he finally wrote to the Christians in the world's capital city, Rome, and then went to live amongst them. And by then, too, his travels had taken him through many of the cities and along many of the roads of the eastern part of the great Roman Empire.

Rome was the third influence which contributed to the make-up of this remarkable man. Strangest of all, it was a Roman citizen who wrote this letter to the Christians in Rome. Not only was Paul born into a strict Jewish family living in a Greek university city and port, his family were also Roman citizens. The nearest comparison for us might be an Indian family which had emigrated from India to West Africa during the days of the British Empire, and had settled down as civil servants. They would retain their religious links with India, but their lives would be deeply influenced by their new background and their responsibilities. If the family was then honoured by the British government, perhaps with a knighthood, the comparison with Paul's family would be complete. We do not know what Paul's father or grandfather had done to deserve it, but he had been made a Roman citizen, and his son or grandson, Paul, inherited the honour.

Roman citizenship was not only an honour, it conferred great privileges as well. In British law a knight or a lord is subject to the same laws and the same courts as anyone else. In the Roman system, citizenship gave a man valuable rights to special treatment. In the harsh world of Roman justice, it protected him from torture, flogging and arbitrary imprisonment if he was suspected of wrongdoing. He was treated with respect and caution by local officials, and given protection if he was in danger. He could even take his case straight to the Emperor himself if he was charged before a local court, wherever it might be, and then the smooth Roman administrative machine would move him to Rome with an army escort to guard and protect him, for the case to be heard in the Emperor's supreme court.

Paul was proud of his Roman citizenship. He even changed over to his Roman name Paullus, instead of his

Jewish name, Saul. He used his citizenship on his travels whenever he needed it. At Philippi, on the second of his Christian missionary journeys through the Near East, Paul and his companion were arrested, flogged and thrown into the town prison for the night. Next morning the local magistrates sent orders for them to be released and sent packing, but Paul would have none of it: 'But Paul said to the police officers, "We are not found guilty of any crime, yet they whipped us in public – and we are Roman citizens! Then they threw us in prison. And now they want to send us away secretly? Not at all! The Roman officials themselves must come here and let us out." The police officers reported these words to the Roman officials; and when they heard that Paul and Silas were Roman citizens, they were afraid. So they went and apologized to them; then they led them out of the prison and asked them to leave the city.' (Acts 16:37-9)

Paul's insistence on his rights would help the small group of Christians in Philippi as their new way of life aroused suspicion and opposition. But it also helps us to understand the confidence with which Paul could write to the Christians of Rome. Although he had never been there, he felt that he was one of them. As a fellow-citizen he knew how they thought and he understood their way of life.

The Jewish way of life, with its great religious traditions. The Greek way of life, with its feeling for truth and beauty. The Roman way of life, with its world-wide vision and its confidence. All these meet in the man who wrote this letter to the Romans.

Before he became a Christian, Paul had a promising career ahead of him as an able Jewish lawyer, administrator and politician. His conversion to the way of life and the teachings of Jesus were to change all that. His abilities were turned in a new direction. Whatever happened to him on the Damascus Road, when he first realized that Jesus, the crucified Galilean peasant, was alive and had come to him, Paul's entire life was changed. Inevitably, Paul went through a period of turmoil during which he retreated into seclusion to sort out his life. Then he directed all his energies towards understanding the Christian way of life, and to spreading it throughout the Roman world.

His letter to the Christians of Rome was written twenty years later, when he was at the height of his work as a Christian leader. Twenty years of experience and thought have gone into the writing of it.

THE READERS

Paul wrote his letter to the Christians in Rome nearly thirty years after the crucifixion of Jesus. What kind of people were those first-generation Christians? What did they think about Jesus Christ? How had they heard about him?

The Romans were a practical people. They were engineers, administrators, soldiers. Whatever theories or views people might hold, in the end they had to work in practice if they were to make much headway in Rome.

By the first century of the Christian era, the city had the best part of a million people living in it. The great network of roads, which fanned out from Rome to every part of her great Empire, brought news, wealth, food and, above all, people pouring into the city. From it there flowed a steady stream of administrators, imperial messengers, soldiers, merchants and travellers of every description. The citizens of Rome could be forgiven for believing that they lived in the most important city in the world.

More than half of Rome's million inhabitants were slaves. Wherever the Roman army conquered, the slave markets were fed with a fresh batch of captives. Debt, famine or a natural disaster would open up the same route to the unfortunate people caught in it, unless they had the precious protection of Roman citizenship. The children of slaves automatically became slaves, and were bred for slavery. Throughout the Empire, the whole economy was built on slave foundations.

Ever since the Spartacus revolt, more than a century earlier, Rome feared a rebellion of the slaves and suppressed any signs of it ruthlessly. Even so, slaves could sometimes rise to positions of great power and luxury, particularly if they were in the Emperor's household. The civil service was mainly staffed by slaves, who could become senior officials in the Emperor's administration. At the other end of the scale, the slaves in the mines were treated as animals, and not very valuable ones at that.

Above the slaves in the social scale were the freemen,

at one time the real power in Rome during the days of the Republic. They were labourers, craftsmen, shop-keepers, or merely unemployed, for the unemployment figures sometimes reached 20% of the total population of Rome. Such was the wealth of the city, and particularly of the Emperor, that the basic necessities of life could be met by free distributions of bread and money. In addition, a complex traditional system of patronage meant that most freemen had a protector higher up the social scale who saw that they did not go short. In turn, they gave their protectors political support. Lavish public games and circuses, freely provided at the expense of the state or of rich Roman nobles, lasted for weeks at a time.

The main profits and the power were in the hands of two grades of noblemen, divided by wealth and birth. The higher grade formed the Senate and from its ranks were drawn the magistrates, higher officers of the army, and the governors of the many provinces of the Empire.

In theory, the whole complex social structure was carefully balanced so that no single class had overall power. In practice, the Emperor wielded absolute power of life and death, with nothing short of assassination as a means of controlling him. Behind the Emperor were the legions. Provided he could keep the army content, the Emperor could do whatever he wanted. When Paul wrote this letter, the Emperor was Nero, aged twenty and supreme ruler of the Roman Empire for four years. Already he had made his mark as a ruthless, debauched and unbelievably vain man.

The city was a maze of narrow winding streets, tall crumbling tenements, and spacious squares with magnifi-cent temples and public buildings. Traffic was forbidden during the day, to keep the streets clear for the throngs that moved through them. At night, the city was filled with the din of the great carts as they ground through the streets. Not even wealth could buy freedom from noise. One thing at least mitigated the tightly packed squalor in which even the free citizens lived: fresh water flowed into the city along aqueducts, from springs thirty miles away, to supply houses and the great public baths. For their roads and their water supply, the Romans were ahead of modern civilization by nearly two thousand years.

Above all, the Romans were traditionalists, reluctant

to abandon anything from their past. The ruthless military machine and the smooth civil service was manned by people who looked to the past for their inspiration. It showed in their religion. The superstitions of a far more primitive age still held sway over the Romans' lives. They examined the entrails of sacrificial animals and watched the flight of birds before doing anything important, to discover whether the time was right for it. A host of minor gods, goddesses and spirits were placated and worshipped, each with its statue, its temple and its priests.

As the legions expanded the Empire into Asia, eastern religions began to gain Roman adherents. They worshipped at the fertility cults and the 'mystery' religions with their secret rites of initiation. The gods and the philosophies of Greece had long since been adopted by the Romans, especially by the educated upper classes, just as most of the doctors were Greeks.

In truth, there was no single dominant religion or faith amongst Romans, except their pride in their city. The basic faith of the Romans was their faith in Rome itself. Their city symbolized a nation which was sure that it was invincible, and that it had a divine right to rule the world.

So what of the Christian community in Rome, twenty-eight years after the crucifixion of Jesus? No one knows for sure when it was founded, or who first took the Christian gospel to Rome. The tradition that it was Peter who did so is very strong, but there is no evidence for it in the New Testament.

Perhaps the best explanation lies in the Roman roads. As the Christian gospel spread in the Greek-speaking countries at the eastern end of the Mediterranean, some of the Romans on their travels would take Christianity back to Rome with them, and so a small Christian group formed in the capital city. In chapter 16 of this letter, Paul shows that he had already met a number of the Christians of Rome, and this could only be while he and they were travelling, for Paul had not visited the city. The normal method used by the apostles to spread the news of Christ was to teach first in a town's Jewish synagogue, where the people would at least understand something of the background for the gospel. This approach had not been used in Rome, for the Jews there knew little about Christianity when Paul finally arrived, three years after his letter (see Acts 28:17-28).

We can only guess at the background of the Christians to whom Paul wrote in Rome. The first Christians held their meetings at night, from sunset on Saturday to sunrise on Sunday, so work or even slavery would not prevent a person attending. The Roman Christians could have been drawn from any class in the city. But whatever their class, they had one thing in common. They were living in circumstances remarkably close to those of modern times.

The politics, the bustle, the complicated structure of a big city were in the air the Romans breathed. They expected to be informed about events all over the vast extent of the Roman Empire, and to be able to go to any corner of it if it was necessary. Even the corn which fed them came from Egypt. They were cosmopolitans, and they would have understood our modern way of life immediately, with all its opportunities, its problems and its complexity. Paul's letter to them sets out the Christian way of life for people like ourselves.

THE LETTER

Paul's letter to the Romans was written near the end of one of the most interesting periods in his life. He wrote it from Corinth, just before returning to Palestine from the third and last of his missionary journeys, but it is Paul's relationship with the Christians of Corinth which helps to make the letter so unusual.

The Christians in Corinth were particularly dear to Paul, but at some stage during the earlier part of this journey he had angered them so much that they were no longer prepared to accept him. He wrote a number of letters to them, two of which (1 and 2 Corinthians) have survived. The first is full of advice and suggestions, but the second letter to the Corinthians shows that Paul had passed through a deeply disturbing experience in his relationship with them. It had taught him much about suffering, and about his responsibilities as an apostle. It forced him to realize how much he needed the love and power of Jesus.

Now he had reached Corinth again, and could relax in his restored and deepened friendship with the Corinthian Christians. His thoughts turned towards Rome, where there was already a Christian church. Paul hoped that he could at last visit the capital of the Empire of which he was proud to be a citizen, perhaps on his next missionary journey, and he now wrote to prepare the way. He even hoped that Rome would become his missionary base, so that he could spread the gospel westwards as far as Spain.

In this letter to the Christians of Rome Paul sets out the Christian gospel and its significance. Although he has never visited these people in their own city, he knows that they will have been taught the same truths as he himself was taught. Paul's letter is an opportunity to take stock, and to assess the progress they have all made in their understanding of the message of salvation during the twenty-eight years which have passed since the crucifixion and resurrection of Jesus Christ.

It is a letter about love. Mankind had got itself into

such a mess that no one could avoid it, or escape from it. Only God has the power to bring the world back into his love again.

The new act of love which saves the world is the life and work of Jesus Christ, for Jesus is the Son of God and all God's love is his to use. Jesus brought the love of God into the world with him, and the innocence, freedom and goodness which every person longs for.

To share in the love of God, all that is needed is to trust entirely in Jesus. The love he shares with people is stronger than death, and it can raise them to the perfection that God wants them to have. God takes the human longing for perfection, no matter how feeble it may be, and he makes it as strong as his own love. Through Jesus, everyone can receive the full love of God, and can return it just as fully. The gap between man and God has been bridged.

Paul had written before about God's love and man's response to it, especially in 1 Corinthians, but in this letter to the Christians in Rome he spells it all out with systematic care. This is the gospel, the Good News, as Paul and his fellow-Christians experienced it in their lives. It was God's love in action, bringing success where all else had failed, and filling the world with hope.

The letter is best read in seven parts. It should be remembered that this is the work of a man who has thought deeply about the Christian faith and has carried heavy responsibilities for other Christians. There is nothing theoretical about it. It was dictated to a man named Tertius, who inserts a brief note of greeting near the end (Romans 16:22).

1. Opening Remarks 1:1-17

Paul sets out his credentials at the beginning, but quickly goes on to write about the grounds of their faith. The gospel ('Good News') rests on Jesus Christ, who was both man and God, and so could bring the world back to God again. Paul's task, as an apostle, is to help bring all people to Jesus. He has already thought this out in 2 Corinthians (see, especially, 2 Corinthians 5:11-6:10).

He thanks God for the Roman Christians, and goes on to sum up the Good News in a brief phrase. It tells how God puts men right with himself. It is by their faith and their relationship with God which grows from it. The next three parts work this out in detail.

2. Universal Guilt and Need 1:18-3:20

Like the author of Genesis 1-11, so many centuries before him, Paul makes a realistic examination of human nature and its achievements, and concludes that it is a history of failure and frustration.

The knowledge of God has been available to everyone. He has revealed himself in nature, and in people's consciences. The great authors and philosophers of the Greek and Roman world show how true this is, yet the pagan peoples have failed to apply their knowledge of God in their lives.

For Jews, it is even worse, for they have also had the special revelation that God has made to them in their history and in their laws, yet they have failed even more completely than the Gentiles. Conscience, nature and the divine law all show how helpless man is when he tries to live by his own strength alone. He has ruined his relationship with God, and is powerless to put it right again. Only God can heal the breach and bring people to the perfection for which he has made them.

3. God's Act of Salvation 3:21-5:11

Jesus Christ is the key figure in God's plan. He is Son of God with all the ultimate love of God which no power can damage or break, and he became man to share that love and to show its strength. In language borrowed from the law courts, from the release of slaves, and from the Hebrew temple sacrifices, Paul shows how he understands the achievement of Jesus. He shares his innocence, his freedom, and his sanctified life with man. The guilty are declared innocent by God; the people enslaved by their own depravity are set free; the consecrated life-force of Jesus, which he shows right through to his death, cleanses people from their sins.

God expresses his love through his Son, and because this is love it works through man's response. The response of faith is to trust in the love and power of God, as it is found in Jesus Christ, and in nothing else. Abraham showed such trust, even when he discovered that he was barren. He trusted that God could bring life out of the death and barrenness of human effort, just as Christians know that God raised Jesus from the dead. The power of life which brought the universe into being has been released into the world again in a new way to bring mankind back to God.

Even the response of faith is aided and amplified by God, for he has poured the Holy Spirit into people's hearts, so that their hopes may be realized.

4. God's Power Overcomes Human Weakness 5:12-8:39

For centuries, men had hoped that the divine law, revealed through Moses, would bring them back to God. But the law only condemned them, and showed them how far they were from deserving God's friendship and love. In Jesus, God has opened a new way of reaching him. He unites people to Jesus, with an unbreakable union which begins with baptism, so that they can share in his death and resurrection.

This does not remove their responsibilities for their lives. But now they are linked with the power of God's love, and response becomes possible at last. In a long and powerful passage (Romans 7), Paul writes movingly about the frustrations which are experienced as the old habits are broken and the new life in Christ takes effect.

Even now, if the new life depended on unaided human response, it would still be impossible, despite the death and resurrection of Jesus. But God sends the Holy Spirit to co-operate with our efforts, and amplify them until they match the love which God gives to us. With the aid of the Spirit, we are able to live as God's children, and know that we share in the glory of Christ as well as his sufferings. Nothing on earth, or afterwards, can ever separate us from love such as this.

5. God's Plan: Jews and Gentiles 9:1-11:36

For three chapters Paul wrestles with the problem of the Jewish people and their place in God's plan. Individual Jews, such as Paul himself, have been taken into the new people of God. But he feels that there must be a time when the whole Jewish people realize that all their history and their past experience has reached its climax in Jesus Christ.

They became set in their ways, and were unable to

recognize the new initiative of God when it came. But God will bring them back to himself again, and their return will deepen the blessings and richness which Christians are already experiencing. Meanwhile, they should be taken as a warning. Their privileged position ended in complacency and rejection, and Christians could commit the same terrible mistakes.

6. Practical Advice for Life in Christ 12:1-15:13

The Christian life has practical consequences, in the way in which Christians treat each other and the people amongst whom they live. Paul develops the insights about the 'body of Christ' – the interdependence of Christians on each other – which he first expressed in 1 Corinthians. He writes about relationships with the secular powers, and it is worth noting that it will be five years before the first serious persecution of Christians by the State begins, when Nero makes the Roman Christians the scapegoats for the great fire of AD 64.

There is a powerful appeal for peace and love amongst Christians, and concern for weaker members. Paul would have vivid memories of the way in which the Christian community in Corinth began to disintegrate, and the selfishness which marked it even in their worship at the Eucharist. Christians must behave towards each other as Christ has behaved towards themselves. No other standard is good enough.

7. Plans, Greetings and Conclusion 15:14-16:27

Paul returns to his plans to visit Rome, and writes about his present task. The collection he is taking back to Palestine is a gift to the Jewish Christians from the Gentile converts. It expresses their union with them in Christ, and their gratitude for the salvation which God has given to them. The Jews played a vital part in that salvation, and the Gentiles are acknowledging it.

Paul sends greetings to the many Christians of Rome whom he has met at various places on his travels, and concludes with a great prayer of thanksgiving to God for their faith. They have discovered the secret truth which was hidden for so long, and which has now been revealed in Jesus Christ. God has won the final battle against evil, and he is bringing his world back to himself again.

Paul's next letters will be from Rome, and they will contain powerful passages about God's great plan and the climax which has been reached in it (see, particularly, Ephesians 1:3-14). But he will be there as a prisoner of the Roman government, waiting for his appeal to be heard by the Emperor Nero.

PAUL'S LETTER TO
THE ROMANS

1 From Paul, a servant of Christ Jesus, and an apostle chosen and called by God to preach his Good News.
²The Good News was promised long ago by God through his prophets, and written in the Holy Scriptures. ³It is about his Son, our Lord Jesus Christ: as to his humanity, he was born a descendant of David; ⁴as to his divine holiness, he was shown with great power to be the Son of God by being raised from death. ⁵Through him God gave me the privilege of being an apostle, for the sake of Christ, in order to lead people of all nations to believe and obey. ⁶This also includes you who are in Rome, whom God has called to belong to Jesus Christ.
⁷And so I write to all of you in Rome whom God loves and has called to be his own people:
May God our Father and the Lord Jesus Christ give you grace and peace.

Prayer of Thanksgiving

⁸First, I thank my God, through Jesus Christ, for all of you; because the whole world is hearing of your faith. ⁹God can prove that what I say is true—the God whom I serve with all my heart by preaching the Good News about his Son. God knows that I always remember you ¹⁰every time I pray. I ask that God, in his good will, may at last make it possible for me to visit you now. ¹¹For I want very much to see you in order to share a spiritual blessing with you, to make you strong. ¹²What I mean is that both you and I will be helped at the same time, you by my faith and I by your faith.
¹³You must remember this, my brothers: many times I have planned to visit you, but something has always kept me from doing so. I want to win converts among you, too, as I have among other Gentiles. ¹⁴For I have an obligation to all peoples, to the civilized and to the savage, to the educated and to the ignorant. ¹⁵So then, I am eager to preach the Good News to you also who live in Rome.

The Power of the Gospel

[16]I have complete confidence in the gospel; it is God's power to save all who believe, first the Jews and also the Gentiles. [17]For the gospel reveals how God puts men right with himself: it is through faith, from beginning to end. As the scripture says, "He who is put right with God through faith shall live."

Section 1: Opening Remarks
Romans 1:1-17

By the time Paul came to write his letter to the Christians in Rome, he had already been working as a Christian leader for at least fifteen years. Church after church in the eastern part of the Roman Empire owed its existence to him. If anyone had doubted his energy and courage, he could have pointed to the many things he had already endured as he travelled through the network of Roman roads, spreading the Good News of Jesus Christ. Not that he set much store by his experience of hardships, but in the last letter he wrote to the Christians in Corinth, immediately before this letter to the Romans, Paul reminded them of what he had been through (2 Corinthians 11:23-9). He was famous amongst all Christians.

Now Paul wanted to extend his work into the western part of the Empire. Rome's rule stretched right through southern Europe to Spain and the Atlantic coast of France. Ten years before Paul wrote this letter, the Roman legions had crossed into Britain and most of it was already firmly under their control. Only the eastern parts of Europe, north of the Danube and east of the Rhine, lay outside the Roman peace.

The opportunity lay wide open. Paul, Roman citizen and outstandingly successful missionary, was the man to see the way ahead. Still only in his forties, he could hope to have spread the Christian message throughout the length of the Roman Empire by the time he died.

Rome must be the base. It was the focus of the great network of roads and the centre of the world. So Paul wrote to the small Christian community in Rome to let them know that he was planning to visit them. He would indeed be welcomed by them.

In his letter to them, Paul shows them why the Good News of Jesus Christ has been such an inspiration to him. It has given him the freedom and the power to respond to God's love. It has opened his eyes to the whole pattern of God's saving power, which reached its climax in the life, death and resurrection of Jesus Christ. It has pointed the way to peace, equality and freedom for all men, as they share in the life of God.

There is nothing here that the Christians in Rome do not know already, but Paul wants them to realize that he shares to the full in their new life. His visit will deepen their faith and his, so that he can use their city as a springboard to bring the whole Roman world to God.

Introductions 1:1-7

Romans is a letter, and like any letter-writer, Paul starts with greetings and a mention of his purpose in writing. But this is more than an ordinary letter for the man who is writing it and the people who are to read it. They know that they are standing at a crossroads in the history of the world. The long centuries have all been moving towards this moment. They feel like someone who has finished his education and can start work at last, or a nation which has been working for many years towards the conquest of space. The rocket has blasted off; the new age has arrived.

A new, world-shaking power has been released into the world, made possible by the life and achievements of Jesus Christ. People are no longer trapped by their own weaknesses and failings. They can now share in the strength of God himself.

Nowadays, we are used to people debunking the great heroes who have made our nation what it is. A Wellington or a Churchill, a Washington or a Roosevelt have to be shown in all their limitations and shortcomings. They are cut down to size. There is no way of doing this with Jesus Christ.

Humanly speaking, Jesus succeeded where kings and rulers had failed. God had intended that King David would be the first of a great line of rulers who would help their people to live in peace and love. They were to be God's representatives, and all the benefits of the covenant

with God would flow through them. In the end, this
would be the way in which the love of God would reach
out to all the peoples of the world. The covenant with
David, described in 2 Samuel 7, was to be the start of it all.

Unfortunately, the kings were too corrupt and weak
for such grave responsibilities. They ruled by the methods
of any other earthly government, and the nation suffered.
In his life on earth, Jesus brought in a new kind of
kingship which showed what God's love really means.
He looked for the good in all men, no matter what
their fellow-men might think of them. He gave people
the value which God puts upon them, and showed them
the respect due to them. Only hypocrisy, injustice and
the prostitution of religion aroused his anger. With that
there could be no compromise, even if it resulted in his
death.

The love by which Jesus lived was stronger than anything which tried to destroy it, even death itself. At last
the world had been shown a new way of life which could
succeed where all human effort brought misery and
suffering.

For Jesus brought to the world a power far beyond
anything it had experienced before. He was the Son of
God. When he became a man at Bethlehem he had laid
aside all the outward signs of his power and his glory, but
the reality of them was still there in all its strength. The
very fact that he had risen to life again after the deadly
efficiency of a Roman execution was proof enough of the
power at work in him.

There is a glimpse here of the driving force which Paul
felt was at work in himself. He represented an irresistible
power for good. He could go with confidence into a
hostile town, and tell them about the new life which God
was offering to them. Like Jesus, he might be ill-treated,
or even killed, but God's love would triumph. Those who
responded to the opportunity Paul offered to them would
discover the power of God's love for themselves.

When John wrote his gospel, he put the work of Jesus
into its true perspective. He started by saying who Jesus
really was. This man who died on a cross amidst the jeers
of the crowd was really the force which had brought
the world into existence, which held it on its course,
which could overcome every power which tried to thwart

God: 'Before the world was created, the Word already existed; he was with God, and he was the same as God. From the very beginning, the Word was with God. Through him God made all things; not one thing in all creation was made without him. The Word was the source of life and this life brought light to men. The light shines in the darkness, and the darkness has never put it out.' (John 1:1-5)

No wonder that a man like Paul was filled with confidence as he went about his work. He was offering people the love which Jesus himself had shown. No power on earth was a match for it. Converting the Roman Empire was only the first step towards converting the world.

Prayer of Thanksgiving 1:8-15

Nationalism is as old as civilization itself. It is as if people need to be limited in their loyalties. The human race is too big and too vague to capture the imagination. People feel that they belong to smaller, clearer groups, perhaps made up of their own 'kith and kin'. As communications have improved, the national unit has grown larger, and people may feel they belong to a whole continent. But the old, narrow loyalties, and the pull of a small district are still strong forces beneath the surface.

The Christian gospel cuts across all human groupings and all national divisions. In the end, it no longer matters what district or what race people belong to. Their importance does not depend on where they happen to have been born, or what they have inherited from their past.

More than once, Paul makes this point in his letters. Christians are a new race, in which all the old divisions have been swept away: 'You have put off the old self with its habits, and have put on the new self. This is the new man which God, its creator, is constantly renewing in his own image, to bring you to a full knowledge of himself. As a result there are no Gentiles and Jews, circumcised and uncircumcised, barbarians, savages, slaves, or freemen, but Christ is all, Christ is in all.' (Colossians 3:9-11)

Rome, with its seething population and its deep class divisions, had great need of this new way of life, and Paul hoped to be able to spread the Christian message throughout the city. But beyond the city lay the Empire, and beyond the Empire the world. Rome was only a beginning, and the power of God's love would transform the world.

The Christians of Rome were to play a vital part in this work, not because they were in any way superior to other Christians, but only through the faith which all Christians should show. Later in his letter, Paul will have much to say about the place of faith, and what it is. Here, as he quietly opens his letter, he is content to say how much he depends on it.

The Christian life is never a solitary one. It creates links between people, links which cut across all other ties. People are strengthened by each other's faith, so that a person is never dependent on the quality of his or her own response alone.

Many times in the gospels, faith is seen as a shared power, a force which can work for the good of others and draw them closer to God. One of the most vivid examples is that of the paralysed man, brought to Jesus by his friends and let down through a hole in the roof of the house where Jesus was teaching. Mark makes it clear that Jesus was moved when he saw this friendship of faith (Mark 2:1-12), and here, as elsewhere, he makes it the background for the power of love.

For all that he seemed to be a self-sufficient man, Paul was never a lone operator. He depended on the sympathy and encouragement of his fellow-Christians. Indeed, when Paul found himself at odds with other Christians in any serious way, it stopped him in his tracks, as had recently happened when he made the Corinthian Christians angry. The support which Christians give to each other is their faith in the power of God's love, shared with each other and amplifying each other's efforts.

Even so, there is just a hint in this passage that his plans to come to Rome might yet again be thwarted. Paul must have known that his opportunities could not last indefinitely. Sooner or later, his enemies amongst his fellow-Jews, or a change of policy in the Roman government, would stop his work. Would it happen before he could reach Rome and extend his work into the West?

The Power of the Gospel 1:16-17

In these brief words, Paul sums up the whole pattern of
God's plan for man and the way in which it works out.
Anyone who understands what is happening realizes that
he or she is in touch with an irresistible force for good.
For centuries past, the Jews had caught glimpses of the
way in which God works, drawing people to himself.

Now the whole pattern has been made clear in the good
news about Jesus Christ. The opportunity is open to
everyone. Whatever has happened to separate people
from God, it has now been put right. God's power
breaks down all barriers, and reaches everyone, no matter
how degraded he may be.

The Christian hope is more than a new piece of information or a new method of thought. It is power.
Earlier, in 1 Corinthians, Paul had spelled this out. There
have been many philosophical systems which have offered
happiness, but none of them has the power which Jesus
showed in his way of life. Even if such an approach to
life leads to suffering and death, the people who try it
discover that it has a power about it which makes it
supremely convincing. They find that they are sharing in
the risen life of Jesus, so that suffering and death no
longer defeat them. It shows them that God's love is
stronger than any human strength.

The Christian way confers ultimate strength, but only
to those who trust it completely. It saves, but it can only
do so when it meets with the full response of faith. There
is nothing automatic about God's power; it does not
overwhelm human freedom. It is love, which works by
free co-operation of the ones who are loved. Those who
are loved must have faith in the lover if they are going to
benefit from his love.

This pattern of love, the demonstration of how love
works, can be seen in the encounters people have with
Jesus in the gospels. They are never forced by him. If they
do not really trust him, he can do nothing to help them.
If they will not accept that he has extraordinary powers of
love, his love cannot reach them. It is even possible that
they will explain his love away as an evil power, because
they fear that it will change their own way of life. Some
of the religious leaders produced this explanation when

they thought that their position was threatened (Mark 3:22-30). God can only convince people who are willing to be convinced.

Faith is man's response to God's love, and in that response more and more of the love is discovered. There is real progress here. The smallest response, provided it is genuine, is sufficient to start it all. Then as the love is recognized so the faith grows and the trust becomes more complete. If this is a journey, the first step is sufficient to begin it. With each further step the conviction grows that this is the right way.

Paul clinches his argument with an example from Jewish history. The greatest crisis ever faced by the Jews was the disastrous series of mistakes which ended with the destruction of Jerusalem by the Babylonians. The basic mistake had been to run the nation's affairs by human standards of right and wrong, and human ideas of power and might. The Babylonians showed that they were far more powerful, and that they found the Jews a treacherous people.

As the crisis developed, one of the prophets pointed to another way of life: 'He who is put right with God through faith shall live.' (Habakkuk 2:4) It means looking at the situation from God's point of view. Only then would it make sense. By human standards the solutions may seem absurd, but they are the real solutions which lead to life. Faith gives this point of view. It makes a different kind of sense, and it opens up all the saving power of God's love.

ROMANS 1:18-3:20

The Guilt of Mankind

[18]God's wrath is revealed coming down from heaven upon all the sin and evil of men whose evil ways prevent the truth from being known. [19]God punishes them, because what men can know about God is plain to them. God himself made it plain to them. [20]Ever since God created the world, his invisible qualities, both his eternal power and his divine nature, have been clearly seen. Men can perceive them in the things that God has made.

So they have no excuse at all! ²¹They know God, but they do not give him the honour that belongs to him, nor do they thank him. Instead, their thoughts have become complete nonsense and their empty minds are filled with darkness. ²²They say they are wise, but they are fools; ²³instead of worshipping the immortal God, they worship images made to look like mortal man or birds or animals or reptiles.

²⁴Because men are such fools, God has given them over to do the filthy things their hearts desire, and they do shameful things with each other. ²⁵They ex-

They worship images

change the truth about God for a lie; they worship and serve what God has created instead of the Creator himself, who is to be praised forever! Amen.

²⁶Because men do this, God has given them over to shameful passions. Even the women pervert the natural use of their sex by unnatural acts. ²⁷In the same way the men give up natural sexual relations with women and burn with passion for each other. Men do shameful things with each other, and as a result they themselves are punished as they deserve for their wrongdoing.

²⁸Because men refuse to keep in mind the true

knowledge about God, he has given them over to corrupted minds, so that they do the things that they should not. [29]They are filled with all kinds of wickedness, evil, greed, and vice; they are full of jealousy, murder, fighting, deceit, and malice. They gossip, [30]and speak evil of one another; they are hateful to God, insolent, proud, and boastful; they think of more ways to do evil; they disobey their parents; [31]they are immoral; they do not keep their promises, and they show no kindness or pity to others. [32]They know that God's law says that people who live in this way deserve death. Yet, not only do they continue to do these very things, but they also approve of others who do them.

God's Judgment

2 Do you, my friend, pass judgment on others? You have no excuse at all, whoever you are. For when you judge others, but do the same things that they do, you condemn yourself. [2]We know that God is right when he judges the people who do such things as these. [3]But you, my friend, do these very things yourself for which you pass judgment on others! Do you think you will escape God's judgment? [4]Or perhaps you despise his great kindness, tolerance, and patience. Surely you know that God is kind because he is trying to lead you to repent. [5]But you have a hard and stubborn heart. So then, you are making your own punishment even greater on the Day when God's wrath and right judgments will be revealed. [6]For God will reward every person according to what he has done. [7]Some men keep on doing good, and seek glory, honour, and immortal life; to them God will give eternal life. [8]Other men are selfish and reject what is right, to follow what is wrong; on them God will pour his wrath and anger. [9]There will be suffering and pain for all men who do what is evil, for the Jews first and also for the Gentiles. [10]But God will give glory, honour, and peace to all who do what is good, to the Jews first, and also to the Gentiles. [11]For God judges everyone by the same standard.

[12]The Gentiles do not have the Law of Moses; they sin and are lost apart from the Law. The Jews have the Law; they sin and are judged by the Law. [13]For it is

not by hearing the Law that men are put right with God, but by doing what the Law commands. [14]The Gentiles do not have the Law; but whenever of their own free will they do what the Law commands, they are a law to themselves, even though they do not have the Law. [15]Their conduct shows that what the Law commands is written in their hearts. Their consciences also show that this is true, since their thoughts sometimes accuse them and sometimes defend them. [16]And so, according to the Good News I preach, this is how it will be on that Day when God, through Jesus Christ, will judge the secret thoughts of men.

The Jews and the Law

[17]What about you? You call yourself a Jew; you depend on the Law and boast about God; [18]you know what God wants you to do, and you have learned from the Law to choose what is right; [19]you are sure that you are a guide for the blind, a light for those who are in darkness, [20]an instructor for the foolish, and a teacher for the young. You are certain that in the Law you have the full content of knowledge and of truth. [21]You teach others —why don't you teach yourself? You preach, "Do not steal"—but do you yourself steal? [22]You say, "Do not commit adultery"—but do you commit adultery? You detest idols—but do you rob temples? [23]You boast about having God's law—but do you bring shame on God by breaking his law? [24]The scripture says, "Because of you Jews, the Gentiles speak evil of God's name."

[25]If you obey the Law, your circumcision is of value; but if you disobey the Law, you might as well never have been circumcised. [26]If the Gentile, who is not circumcised, obeys the commands of the Law, will not God regard him as though he were circumcised? [27]And so you Jews will be condemned by the Gentiles, because you break the Law, even though you have it written down and are circumcised, while they obey the Law, even though they are not physically circumcised. [28]After all, who is a real Jew, truly circumcised? Not the man who is a Jew on the outside, whose circumcision is a physical thing. [29]Rather, the real Jew is the man who is a Jew on the inside, that is, whose heart has been circumcised,

which is the work of God's Spirit, not of the written Law. This man receives his praise from God, not from men.

3 Do the Jews have any advantage over the Gentiles, then? Or is there any value in being circumcised? ²Much, indeed, in every way! In the first place, God trusted his message to the Jews. ³What if some of them were not faithful? Does it mean that for this reason God will not be faithful? ⁴Certainly not! God must be true, even though every man is a liar. As the scripture says,

> "You must be shown to be right when you
>   speak;
>   you must win your case when you are
>   being tried."

⁵But what if our doing wrong serves to show up more clearly God's doing right? What can we say? That God does wrong when he punishes us? (I speak here as men do.) ⁶By no means! If God is not just, how can he judge the world?

⁷But what if my untruth serves God's glory by making his truth stand out more clearly? Why should I still be condemned as a sinner? ⁸Why not say, then, "Let us do evil that good may come"? Some people, indeed, have insulted me by accusing me of saying this very thing! They will be condemned, as they should be.

No Man Is Righteous

⁹Well then, are we Jews in any better condition than the Gentiles? Not at all! I have already shown that Jews and Gentiles alike are all under the power of sin. ¹⁰As the Scriptures say:

> "There is no one who is righteous,
> ¹¹   no one who understands,
>   or who seeks for God.
> ¹² All men have turned away from God;
>   they have all gone wrong;
>   no one does what is good, not even one.
> ¹³ Their mouths are like an open grave;
>   wicked lies roll off their tongues,
>   and deadly words, like snake's poison,
>   from their lips;

¹⁴   their mouths are full of bitter curses.
¹⁵ They are quick to hurt and kill;
¹⁶   they leave ruin and misery wherever
        they go.
¹⁷ They have not known the path of peace,
¹⁸   nor have they learned to fear God."
¹⁹Now we know that everything in the Law applies to those who live under the Law, in order to stop all human excuses and bring the whole world under God's judgment. ²⁰Because no man is put right in God's sight by doing what the Law requires; what the Law does is to make man know that he has sinned.

Section 2: Universal Guilt and Need
Romans 1:18-3:20

When the story of a great rescue is told, it means nothing unless there is a description of the situation before the rescue started. The camera must move amongst the wrecked houses and show the damage caused by the earthquake if we are to appreciate how much was done to build the city again.

Along with the privileges and responsibilities given to mankind by God, there has also been a grave risk. There was always the possibility that people would try to live without God, or would judge their responsibilities and duties by their own idea of right and wrong. Then there would be chaos. The harmony of the creation would be destroyed, and no power on earth could restore it again.

This is the picture which Paul paints in this section of his letter. From the beginning, people have been able to find out what God wants them to do. He has shown them his goodness and his power. Through their own conscience, and through the way of life he revealed to the Jews, God has shown everyone how to live in his love. But they have ignored him, and then found that they have made a world of hatred and confusion. Only God could rescue them from their misery, and this is why his Son, Jesus Christ, came to earth. It was a rescue operation, a new creation, a chance to start again and rebuild with God's plans and God's power.

In his descriptions, Paul draws on his own experience and the conditions of the world around him, but it is not difficult to transfer his words into our own times and circumstances. There is nothing about the twentieth century which contradicts Paul's picture of human life when it is lived without God.

The Guilt of Mankind 1:18-32

We live in an age of great optimism, at least in the western world. For most people it is a prosperous society in which the basic human needs are secure and many luxuries are easily available. Medical services, housing, food, social security, public services, education and even adequate opportunity for employment can be taken for granted.

That may seem a complacent picture, and an unrealistic one in view of the industrial unrest, and of the complaints of crime, injustice and inefficiency which fill the news. But it is a true picture. Western Europe and North America have a standard of living far higher than most of the world can ever hope for.

We live in a world which places unbounded confidence in man's wisdom and the steady progress of civilization. Each new technological advance feeds this optimism, whether it is the conquest of space or the skill to transplant hearts. Yet this century has seen more bloodshed and inhumanity than any other period in human history. The technological advances have also increased the efficiency with which people can express their hatred and enmity of each other. Some of the bloodiest crimes of all have been committed in this century by nations with the most impressive records for culture.

Paul lived in a world very like our own. Its technology was outstanding, so that even the ruins of its buildings and roads still excite our admiration. We are still watching the plays that Paul might have seen, and reading the authors and poets which he admired. The philosophers of Paul's time are as influential now as they were then. But at heart his world was corrupt. Rome lived by false ideas which could not give people their true dignity and value. The 'climate of opinion' was formed in fear and selfishness, which made people look on others as so many threats to their prosperity and security. In the end, it was might and force which decided who was right. The person, or the group, which could bring most pressure to bear had its own way.

Even ancient Roman religion was based on fear and uncertainty. Every human activity, and every department of life was controlled by a separate god or spiritual power. Success and security depended on knowing which god to placate and the proper rituals for warding off evil influences. A mistake in a sacrifice, or the irrational displeasure of any of the gods, could lead to disaster.

For Paul, there was a terrible stupidity about it all, for the truth was freely available. The world itself was sufficient evidence for the truth about God, if men would only look at it. Despite the misery and injustice which mankind has produced, the goodness and the power of God can still be seen in his creation.

For centuries before Paul's time, great philosophers and poets had been trying to tell people the truth about God and the consequences for human behaviour. Quite apart from any special revelations to the Jews, such Greek philosophers as Socrates, Plato, Aristotle and many others had been teaching and writing about God. But they had been ignored by most of the people of their time.

Whatever the truth and knowledge of God that was available, people preferred to go their own way. In doing so, they were turning away from the only power which could save them from failure and unhappiness. Their lives disintegrated and they found that they were unable to put things right again.

By the time people discovered their mistake it was too late and they were inextricably entangled in a mesh of selfishness and wickedness. Worse still, they might not even be able to recognize their helplessness, but think that this way of life is the normal one for human beings, and even approve of it.

'God's wrath' may seem a strange phrase, but it is Paul's vivid way of saying that God cannot tolerate such wickedness in his creation. Humanly speaking, such a state should lead to punishment and death. But God does not fit into merely human ideas of justice. He rejects totally the corruption of mankind, but he acts to save

men from the misery which they have brought upon
themselves.

God's Judgement 2:1-16

God, in his patient love, continually offers people the
chance of returning to him. Later in this letter, Paul will
show how they can take advantage of this chance, even
though they are too weak to return to God by their own
efforts. But now Paul is dealing with another point.
There is a danger that God's patience may be inter-
preted as tolerance of their wickedness.

Nearly all human comparisons break down when they
are used to describe this patience of God's. Any idea of a
contract or an agreement between God and man fails
here, for human agreements are void when they are
broken, and the obligation to keep the contract ceases –
at least as far as the innocent party is concerned. But
God remains faithful to his promises, no matter how often
man breaks his obligations towards him.

The only comparisons which are at all adequate are all
drawn from human love: the love of parents for children,
which can go far beyond any question of strict justice;
or love between husband and wife, in which one can continue to long for the other to return and renew the
marriage, no matter how serious the breach may have
been.

This point is made in the gospels by many of the
parables which Jesus told, such as the Lost Sheep, the
Lost Coin, and the Lost (Prodigal) Son (Luke 15:4-32).

Eight centuries earlier, the prophet Hosea had made
the same discovery when his marriage was shattered by
his unfaithful wife. Despite her public betrayal of him,
Hosea found that he would still do anything to change
her and bring her back, so that she could discover her
true happiness in the renewed marriage. He realized that
his feelings must be a pale reflection of the feelings God
had towards his unfaithful people (Hosea 2):

'I will betroth you to myself for ever,
  betroth you with integrity and justice,
  with tenderness and love;
I will betroth you to myself with faithfulness,
  and you will come to know the Lord.' (Hosea 2:21-2)

Even so, there is a responsibility laid on those who wish
to live within God's love. It cannot be effective unless
they are willing to return to him. And if they condemn
others while they themselves remain in their wickedness,
they must expect no mercy from God. They show that
they know what is right, and they feel that they have a
duty to take others to task, yet they fail themselves.
Their own forgiveness must be reflected in their forgiveness of others. Their knowledge of their own weakness
must lead them to be sympathetic towards the weaknesses of others. It is hardness and stubbornness which
separate people from God.

In the Lord's Prayer, forgiveness is conditional:
'Forgive us the wrongs that we have done, as we forgive
the wrongs that others have done us' (Matthew 6:12),
and it is this point alone which Jesus emphasized immediately afterwards. The parable of the Unforgiving
Servant makes the same point (Matthew 18:21-35).

At the end of this section of his letter, Paul points out
to his readers that everyone knows the truth about right
and wrong. They do not need to know the law, nor to
have read the great philosophers. Their conscience tells
them whether their actions are acceptable to God or not.
God's way of life 'is written in their hearts'. He gives
them every opportunity to know him and to respond to
his love.

In the end, this personal knowledge will be the only
test of their acceptance or rejection of God. Have they
been faithful to their own deep understanding of what is
really right or wrong, or have they ignored this inner
knowledge? Nothing could be fairer than that.

The Jews and the Law 2:17-3:8

Paul now turns to his own race, the Jews, who have been
privileged with special opportunities to know God. For
more than eighteen hundred years, at least from the time
of Abraham, the Hebrew people claimed to have a special
relationship with God. They called it 'covenant'.

The moment when they really learned what covenant
meant came during their escape from Egypt, in the
thirteenth century BC. From slavery and forced labour,
they were transformed into a free people with a land of
their own, and they were convinced that the power of

their God had done it for them. He had saved them because he loved them, when they had no power to save themselves.

When he delivered them, God had shown the value that he placed on each of them. Consequently, they must recognize God's value in each other, and this must be reflected in all of their relationships with each other. The love and faithfulness of God was to be the basic principle of all their laws.

The Jews were proud of the Law, which they believed had been given to Moses directly by God himself in the desert, immediately after the escape from Egypt (see Exodus 19-24). God made himself known to them in the Law, and guaranteed that his covenant with them would last for ever. There was even a belief amongst many Jews that if the Law was kept perfectly by·all Jews for even one day, God would come in triumph, bring the world to an end and take his people to share in his glory.

They were to be a bridgehead in the world for God, a place where his sovereign authority was recognized and where his love was supreme. All nations would see how attractive God is, and would be drawn to him through the wonderful lives of his servants, the Jews.

It did not work out like that. In fact, the very opposite effect was created. People saw how the Jews broke their divine law, no matter how high their claims might be, and they concluded that the Jewish God must be without any power and no different from their own gods.

Later in this letter (in Romans 7-8), Paul will show that the Law is not enough, no matter how inspiring it might be. In fact, its main effect is to show the Jews how bad they are, just as a perfect piece of workmanship shows up the shoddiness of everything which does not come up to its standard. For many years, Paul himself had depended on the Law, and could speak from his own experience of the frustration of trying to keep it. Wonderful though it was, it did not bring people back to God.

It is always a temptation to try to express religion by laws, and then hope that people will be saved by keeping the laws of the religion. Love is deeper than law, and has power where law fails. To try to live by law is only to experience failure, even if it does make the ideal clearer.

God would indeed be unjust if this was the hope he

held out to his world. He is not that kind of God. Man's wickedness is not a dark background to show God's goodness more clearly. It is a tragedy which God will put right. The solution will flow from his love, in an entirely new way which could never be achieved through the law.

No Man is Righteous 3:9-20

Paul's description of the human need is nearly complete. He has looked at the three ways in which information about God can be obtained, and each of them has proved to be powerless to bring people back to God. Human reason can indeed discover, from an examination of the creation, that there is a supremely good God who is the source of all goodness and truth. The dream of sharing in this ultimate perfection has been held out to mankind by wise men down through the ages and across the breadth of the world, but their vision has made the world no better.

Each individual human being, no matter how insignificant he or she may be, or how far they may be from human standards of civilization, has a personal knowledge of God through conscience. The way to God is planted deep in human nature but it cannot move anyone to travel any nearer to God. The long centuries of special revelation, summarized in all the magnificent detail of the Law of Moses, has made the Jews no better than anyone else. It has even brought God into contempt amongst the rest of mankind.

All that knowledge about God and his goodness has had but one effect. It has shown people how far they are from God and how helpless they are. But it is a beginning. Once people know their need, they are prepared to accept help. They will take the way which God offers to them, the way which only God can offer to them. He has provided a solution, through the life, death and new life of his Son, Jesus Christ. God, in his infinite and patient love, has acted.

How God Puts Men Right

²¹But now God's way of putting men right with himself has been revealed, and it has nothing to do with law. The Law and the prophets gave their witness to it: ²²God puts men right through their faith in Jesus Christ. God does this to all who believe in Christ, because there is no difference at all: ²³all men have sinned and are far away from God's saving presence. ²⁴But by the free gift of God's grace they are all put right with him through Christ Jesus, who sets them free. ²⁵God offered him so that by his death he should become the means by which men's sins are forgiven, through their faith in him. God did this in order to demonstrate his righteousness. In the past, he was patient and overlooked men's sins; ²⁶but now in the present time he deals with men's sins, to demonstrate his righteousness. In this way God shows that he himself is righteous and that he puts right everyone who believes in Jesus.

²⁷What, then, can we boast about? Nothing! And what is the reason for this? Is it that we obey the Law? No, but that we believe. ²⁸For we conclude that a man is put right with God only through faith, and not by doing what the Law commands. ²⁹Or is God only the God of the Jews? Is he not the God of the Gentiles also? Of course he is. ³⁰God is one, and he will put the Jews right with himself on the basis of their faith, and the Gentiles right through their faith. ³¹Does this mean that we do away with the Law by this faith? No, not at all; instead, we uphold the Law.

The Example of Abraham

4 What shall we say, then, of Abraham, our racial ancestor? What was his experience? ²If he was put right with God by the things he did, he would have something to boast about. But he cannot boast before God. ³The scripture says, "Abraham believed God, and because of his faith God accepted him as righteous." ⁴A man who works is paid; his wages are not regarded as a gift, but as something that he has earned. ⁵But the man

who has faith, not works, who believes in the God who declares the guilty to be innocent, it is his faith that God takes into account in order to put him right with himself. [6]This is what David meant when he spoke of the happiness of the man whom God accepts as righteous, apart from any works:

[7] "Happy are those whose wrongs God has
     forgiven,
   whose sins he has covered over!
[8] Happy is the man whose sins the Lord will
     not keep account of!"

[9]Does this happiness that David spoke of belong only to those who are circumcised? No. It belongs also to those who are not circumcised. For we have quoted the scripture, "Abraham believed God, and because of his faith God accepted him as righteous." [10]When did this take place? Was it before or after Abraham was circumcised? Before, not after. [11]He was circumcised later, and his circumcision was a sign to prove that because of Abraham's faith God had accepted him as righteous before he had been circumcised. And so Abraham is the spiritual father of all who believe in God and are accepted as righteous by him, even though they are not circumcised. [12]He is also the father of those who are circumcised, not just because they are circumcised, but because they live the same life of faith that our father Abraham lived before he was circumcised.

God's Promise Received through Faith

[13]God promised Abraham and his descendants that the world would belong to him. This promise was made, not because Abraham obeyed the Law, but because he believed and was accepted as righteous by God. [14]For if what God promises is to be given to those who obey the Law, then man's faith means nothing and God's promise is worthless. [15]The Law brings God's wrath; but where there is no law, there is no disobeying of the law.

[16]The promise was based on faith, then, in order that the promise should be guaranteed as God's free gift to all of Abraham's descendants—not just those who obey the Law, but also those who believe as Abraham did. For Abraham is the spiritual father of us all; [17]as the scrip-

ture says, "I have made you father of many nations." So
the promise is good in the sight of God, in whom Abraham believed—the God who brings the dead to life and
whose command brings into being what did not exist.
[18]Abraham believed and hoped, when there was no
hope, and so became "the father of many nations." Just
as the scripture says, "Your descendants will be this
many." [19]He was almost one hundred years old; but his
faith did not weaken when he thought of his body, which
was already practically dead, or of the fact that Sarah
could not have children. [20]His faith did not leave him,
and he did not doubt God's promise; his faith filled him
with power, and he gave praise to God. [21]He was abso-
lutely sure that God would be able to do what he had
promised. [22]That is why Abraham, through faith, "was
accepted as righteous by God." [23]The words "he was
accepted as righteous" were not written for him alone.
[24]They were written also for us who are to be accepted
as righteous, who believe in him who raised Jesus our
Lord from death. [25]He was given over to die because of
our sins, and was raised to life to put us right with God.

Right with God

5 Now that we have been put right with God through
faith, we have peace with God through our Lord
Jesus Christ. [2]He has brought us, by faith, into this
experience of God's grace, in which we now live. We
rejoice, then, in the hope we have of sharing God's
glory! [3]And we also rejoice in our troubles, because we
know that trouble produces endurance, [4]endurance
brings God's approval, and his approval creates hope.
[5]This hope does not disappoint us, because God has
poured out his love into our hearts by means of the Holy
Spirit, who is God's gift to us.

[6]For when we were still helpless, Christ died for the
wicked, at the time that God chose. [7]It is a difficult thing
for someone to die for a righteous person. It may be that
someone might dare to die for a good person. [8]But God
has shown us how much he loves us; it was while we
were still sinners that Christ died for us! [9]By his death
we are now put right with God; how much more, then,
will we be saved by him from God's wrath. [10]We were

God's enemies, but he made us his friends through the death of his Son. Now that we are God's friends, how much more will we be saved by Christ's life! ¹¹But that is not all; we rejoice in God through our Lord Jesus Christ, who has now made us God's friends.

Section 3: God's Act of Salvation

Romans 3:21-5:11

In the first part of this letter, Paul has examined the human situation realistically. Whenever man has attempted to live without God he has only discovered how helpless he is. All human beings can discover God, and can know what kind of action will bring them close to God. The world of nature and their own consciences tell men and women about God and about the good life which leads to satisfaction and happiness. Jews have the further advantage of their history and their laws, in which God has made himself known in a special way.

Yet every nation and every generation has failed to show God's love and to achieve the perfection for which they are made. In the end, all human effort disintegrates and shows how helpless human beings are. Paul has only repeated the lesson which was first discovered by the author of the opening chapters of Genesis. By arrogance and a mistaken independence, mankind has damaged its relationship with God, and only God can put it right again.

In his generous love, God acts to restore the relationship, by the life and work of his Son, Jesus Christ. Jesus is the only man who is truly innocent, free and united with God. In his life on earth, his death and resurrection, he shows that his innocence, his freedom and his union with God cannot be broken. God gives his Son, so that man can share in his sonship and be cleansed from all sins.

All that is needed on man's part is trust in Jesus. If man trusts to his own abilities he will only fail; the law can only condemn and prove that human beings fall far short of God's love. But God has provided the answer, and it only remains for man to respond to God's love by depending solely on the saving power of Jesus Christ.

This is faith. Abraham showed it when he trusted in God's promises and God's way of working. Even when he discovered that both he and his wife were barren, he was confident that God could bring life out of death and create a nation which would be faithful to him. Circumcision was the sign given to Abraham and his descendants, but it was to remind them they were chosen because of their faith. If they thought that their birth conferred an automatic privilege they would only experience failure and frustration again.

Even this response to God's saving love would be impossible for man. But God has given the Holy Spirit, to make it possible for man to respond and to grow into the fulness of love. We were enemies of God. He has removed the enmity and gone farther. We share in the life of Christ and are raised into the fullest possible friendship with God.

How God Puts Men Right 3:21-31

Paul has established the background for God's supreme act of love. By trying to live without God, mankind has only demonstrated its weakness and helplessness. If there is to be any future, let alone salvation, for man, the initiative must come from God. The law is ineffective as a force for good: it can only set the standards and show how far men fall short of them.

The action taken by God is a new one, yet it is also a development of the action taken by God throughout the period of the Old Testament. 'The Law and the prophets' is the Hebrew title for the greater part of the Old Testament, and covers the first five books, history books and all of the teachings of the prophets. From the earliest times, the Hebrews discovered that their lives disintegrated whenever they ignored their God and the principles by which he had taught them to live. Yet he never deserted them. Time and again, and particularly at the great escape from Egypt when he established his covenant with the whole people, God had rescued them from their helplessness.

Now God had acted again, but this time he had sent his Son, Jesus Christ, to perform the decisive act of salvation. There is no question of mankind earning or deserving such an act of love from God; the failure and the guilt is universal. But Jesus Christ was sent by God to repair the breach between man and God, and to bring all men to the perfection for which God has made them.

Paul uses three examples from everyday life to explain what has happened. 'God puts men right' and 'they are all put right' is a phrase drawn from the law courts. It is the moment when the court delivers its verdict, and in this case the verdict is 'not guilty'. Despite the admission of universal guilt, God acts to make the prisoner innocent, and he is released from his imprisonment.

'Sets them free' has its origins in the freeing of a slave or the release of a soldier from his military service. The slave who has been born into slavery, or has had to sell himself, and the soldier drafted into the army, are both of them at the mercy of their masters and their superiors. God gives them control over their own lives again.

'So that by his death he should become the means by which men's sins are forgiven' refers to the practice of sacrifice, which was the normal way of worship for everyone in the ancient world, whatever religion they professed.

There is a danger, here, that the phrase might be read in a pagan sense, for many pagan religions taught that sacrifices were made to satisfy the anger of the gods, or to substitute another victim. But for Jews, sacrifice was above all a way of entering into communion with God. The blood of the 'victim' was filled with the life and power of God, and it cleansed the worshippers when it was sprinkled on them.

The death of Jesus was the supreme moment when he showed that nothing could make him turn away from God. God's love, in Jesus Christ, is stronger than any of the destructive powers of sin, and it is this which cleanses men from their sins. In the original Greek, Paul wrote that God had offered Christ 'to cleanse by his blood', to show that he was faithful to his promises. Christ's blood is the power of God's love.

God has acted for the salvation of man, and this time he has done so decisively. Mankind is offered a share in the innocence, the freedom and the perfect life of love which Jesus possesses as Son of God.

For this supreme offer of love to be effective, there must

be a response by man. Paul will deal with this in the next section; here it is sufficient to say that this response is faith. There must be faith in the love of God as it is shown in Jesus Christ; utter trust and dependence on the power of God to save. And it must be coupled with the realization that without God man is utterly helpless.

The images and examples are just as valid today as they were in Paul's day, and provided they are used as pointers into the mystery of Christ's saving love, rather than definitions, they can still help us to understand God's impact on our lives.

The drama of the law courts still means freedom or ruin to those who are in the dock, according to the way the verdict goes. There is no slick lawyer to baffle the court or produce last-minute evidence of man's innocence in God's court. Yet we are allowed to share in the innocence of God's own Son, the only man ever to have been innocent in this world.

In our society of mortgages and debts, there can be few who do not feel the force of an act which would free them from their burdens and give them the chance to live the lives they would really plan for themselves. Re-demption is just such an idea, except that it releases people for the perfection which alone can give them absolute satisfaction. They are free to love, in Christ, even as they are loved by God.

More than any other image, new life most captures the imagination. It is what the child receives from the parent, the lover from the beloved. It is the supreme gift given by God as he grants his people a limitless share in the risen life of Jesus.

All of them are positive ideas. Innocence, freedom, new life, are all opportunities which open out endless vistas of the kingdom of God in which love is supreme.

The Example of Abraham 4:1-12

Paul now uses Abraham as a model of the kind of faith which enables a person to benefit from the saving work of Christ. He believed in God's power; he accepted the way in which God exercised it; and he was convinced that there was no other way of achieving his own destiny. God accepted Abraham, and worked through him, solely because Abraham trusted him, not because of any achievement or ability.

God 'declares the guilty to be innocent', and it is precisely the guilty who have nothing to offer to God as the price of his favour. There can only be trust, and gratitude for the unmerited forgiveness which God gives.

The Jews of Paul's time would have accepted that Abraham was their ideal, but they seem to have seen him as the guarantee of their own security. The promises made to Abraham, they thought, were theirs by right because they were descended from him. Jesus rebuked them for such an irresponsible attitude, and warned them that it showed them to be no better than unresponsive rocks (Luke 3:8).

Paul here counters this attitude by pointing out that the mark of circumcision was given to Abraham *after* he had been accepted by God; any man who depends on his circumcision (the sign of his descent from Abraham) for his acceptance by God has made a terrible mistake. And by the same argument, Abraham is the father of all who trust in God, and not merely of those who are physically descended from him. A person cannot be born into a right relationship with God.

It may seem a childish mistake to make, yet it is one which very many people make today about Christianity. At least in the western world, we readily assume that we are Christians through being born into a 'Christian' society, and absorbing Christian values naturally from our parents, our schools and the people we meet.

A white skin, and western culture have become the equivalents of Jewish circumcision. The response to God's love has to be an individual one and a personal one. Without it, the love of God can be as ineffective as it was for the people who sent Jesus to his cross.

God's Promise Received through Faith 4:13-25

In this passage, Paul tackles the problem of the Law, and Christians who still think that their salvation is a reward for their success in keeping the divine Law. This was a belief which recurred throughout New Testament times, and which would make Christianity no more helpful than Judaism had been. No one is able to keep the divine Law, if it is seen as a comprehensive set of rules for the good life. So anyone who bases his or her hopes on their conformity to the Law is bound to be condemned.

Abraham's faith is the key, again, to Christian faith. God's plan, through Abraham, was to create a faithful nation from Abraham's descendants, so that the knowledge of God could grow from generation to generation. But Abraham discovered that his wife was barren. In the end, Abraham accepted that God could give them a child, even though all human effort had failed, and Paul sees this as a model example of faith in God's power.

In fact, Paul is here giving Abraham rather more credit than the account in Genesis, where Abraham and Sarah only accept God's miraculous way for them after they have adopted Abraham's son Ishmael, which was born to Sarah's slave, Hagar. But the main point is clear, and Paul sees Abraham's faith as trust in 'the God who brings the dead to life'. Christian faith is trust in the power of the resurrection of Christ, and certainly not in any human ability to satisfy God's standards.

The mistake of reducing religion to sets of rules and religious customs can be made just as easily today as in New Testament times. Whenever faith is judged by the satisfactory performance of 'religious obligations' the danger is there, and every major Christian church behaves in a way which lays it open to this danger. Response to God's love cannot be measured in terms of attendance at church or the proportion of income distributed in alms.

Faith springs from the realization of personal helplessness, and of God's miraculous love, which brings life out of death and coaxes love from human lovelessness. No laws or regulations can set limits to the response to such love, and no standards can measure it.

Right with God 5:1-11

This section sums up the whole process of salvation. Christ has put us right with God, and our acceptance of this and trust in the love of God has brought us into God's favour.

The proof of it is the experience of coping with problems and troubles which would otherwise be overwhelming. Paul's experiences as an apostle must be in his mind here, and the passages of the letter he had so recently written to the Corinthians (see 2 Corinthians 4:7-6:10).

The hope which this experience generates will be fulfilled, for God has given the Holy Spirit.

This aspect of God's saving power is essential to the total plan of salvation, for man could still be frustrated by his inability to respond to God's love. In the phrase 'God has poured out his love into our hearts' the heart symbolizes the fundamental source of all human action as the mysterious centre of personality.

God places the irresistible power of his love at the disposal of human beings, and makes it effective at the point where they generate their response to him. Paul will work this out in much greater detail later in this letter (see 8:1-30). At this stage, it is sufficient that Paul mentions this final phase in God's saving action, to show how completely God's plan of salvation meets human needs.

God's action, in Jesus Christ and the Holy Spirit, is far more than the removal of enmity. It confers all the positive privileges of friendship, by the share which it gives in the life of his Son, Jesus Christ. Later, Paul will take this to its logical conclusion: we are the children of God, sharing in the glory of Christ himself (8:17).

The references to the Holy Spirit being poured into our hearts echo Old Testament passages about the new covenant, which will be effective where the old covenant failed. Two such passages are Jeremiah 31:31-4 and Ezekiel 36:22-36, both of them written at a time when all attempts to reform the Hebrews had failed and it seemed that they were helpless in their attempts to respond to God's covenant with them.

In every age there is a danger that religion will become fossilized. New situations, and new strains on human relationships, call for new discoveries in religion. Again and again, a generation discovers the relevance of faith to its needs.

The tragedy comes when the new discoveries have become the old banalities. Prayers which once were filled with life are handed on as empty phrases for repetition. Forms of worship which spoke to men's hearts became empty ritual. Doctrines which inspired a generation of Christians are seen as empty formulae in a catechism. In every generation, there is no religion unless it is generated in men's hearts.

ROMANS 5:12-8:39

Adam and Christ

[12]Sin came into the world through one man, and his sin brought death with it. As a result, death spread to the whole human race, because all men sinned. [13] here was sin in the world before the Law was given, but where there is no law, no account is kept of sins. [14]But from the time of Adam to the time of Moses death ruled over all men, even over those who did not sin as Adam did by disobeying God's command.

Adam was a figure of the one who was to come. [15]But the two are not the same, because God's free gift is not like Adam's sin. It is true that many men died because of the sin of that one man. But God's grace is much greater, and so is his free gift to so many men through the grace of the one man, Jesus Christ. [16]And there is a difference between God's gift and the sin of one man. After the one sin came the judgment of "Guilty"; but after so many sins comes the undeserved gift of "Not guilty!" [17]It is true that through the sin of one man death began to rule, because of that one man. But how much

One righteous act sets all men free and gives them life

greater is the result of what was done by the one man, Jesus Christ! All who receive God's abundant grace and the free gift of his righteousness will rule in life through Christ.

¹⁸So then, as the one sin condemned all men, in the same way the one righteous act sets all men free and gives them life. ¹⁹And just as many men were made sinners as the result of the disobedience of one man, in the same way many will be put right with God as the result of the obedience of the one man.

²⁰Law was introduced in order to increase wrongdoing; but where sin increased, God's grace increased much more. ²¹So then, just as sin ruled by means of death, so also God's grace rules by means of righteousness, leading us to eternal life through Jesus Christ our Lord.

Set free from the power of sin

Dead to Sin but Alive in Christ

6 What shall we say, then? That we should continue to live in sin so that God's grace will increase? ²Certainly not! We have died to sin—how then can we go on living in it? ³For surely you know this: when we were baptized into union with Christ Jesus, we were baptized into union with his death. ⁴By our baptism,

then, we were buried with him and shared his death, in order that, just as Christ was raised from death by the glorious power of the Father, so also we might live a new life.

⁵For if we became one with him in dying as he did, in the same way we shall be one with him by being raised to life as he was. ⁶And we know this: our old being has been put to death with Christ on his cross, in order that the power of the sinful self might be destroyed, so that we should no longer be the slaves of sin. ⁷For when a person dies he is set free from the power of sin. ⁸If we have died with Christ, we believe that we will also live with him. ⁹For we know that Christ has been raised from death and will never die again—death has no more power over him. ¹⁰The death he died was death to sin, once and for all; and the life he now lives is life to God. ¹¹In the same way you are to think of yourselves as dead to sin but alive to God in union with Christ Jesus.

¹²Sin must no longer rule in your mortal bodies, so that you obey the desires of your natural self. ¹³Nor must you surrender any part of yourselves to sin, to be used for wicked purposes. Instead, give yourselves to God, as men who have been brought from death to life, and surrender your whole being to him to be used for righteous purposes. ¹⁴Sin must not rule over you; you do not live under law but under God's grace.

Slaves of Righteousness

¹⁵What, then? Shall we sin, because we are not under law but under God's grace? By no means! ¹⁶Surely you know that when you surrender yourselves as slaves to obey someone, you are in fact the slaves of the master you obey—either of sin, which results in death, or of obedience, which results in being put right with God. ¹⁷But thanks be to God! For at one time you were slaves to sin; but then you obeyed with all your heart the truths found in the teaching you received. ¹⁸You were set free from sin and became the slaves of righteousness. ¹⁹I use ordinary words because of the weakness of your natural selves. At one time you surrendered yourselves entirely as slaves to impurity and wickedness, for wicked pur-

poses. In the same way you must now surrender your-selves entirely as slaves of righteousness, for holy purposes. [20]When you were the slaves of sin, you were free from righteousness. [21]What did you gain from doing the things that you are ashamed of now? The result of those things is death! [22]But now you have been set free from sin and are the slaves of God; your gain is a life fully dedicated to him, and the result is eternal life. [23]For sin pays its wage—death; but God's free gift is eternal life in union with Christ Jesus our Lord.

An Illustration from Marriage

7 Certainly you understand what I am about to say, my brothers, because all of you know about law. The law rules over a man only as long as he lives. [2]A married woman, for example, is bound by the law to her husband as long as he lives; but if he dies, then she is free from the law that bound her to him. [3]So then, if she lives with another man while her husband is alive, she will be called an adulteress; but if her husband dies, she is legally a free woman, and does not commit adultery if she marries another man. [4]That is the way it is with you, my brothers. You also have died, as far as the Law is concerned, because you are part of the body of Christ; and now you belong to him who was raised from death in order that we might be useful in the service of God. [5]For when we lived according to our human nature, the sinful desires stirred up by the Law were at work in our bodies, and we were useful in the service of death. [6]Now, how-ever, we are free from the Law, because we died to that which once held us prisoners. No longer do we serve in the old way of a written law, but in the new way of the Spirit.

Law and Sin

[7]What shall we say, then? That the Law itself is sinful? Of course not! But it was the Law that made me know what sin is. I would not have known what it is to covet if the Law had not said, "Do not covet." [8]Sin found its chance to stir up all kinds of covetousness in me by working through the commandment. For sin is a dead

thing apart from law. ⁹I myself was once alive apart from law; but when the commandment came, sin sprang to life, ¹⁰and I died. And the commandment which was meant to bring life, in my case brought death. ¹¹Sin found its chance and deceived me by working through the commandment; by means of the commandment sin killed me.

¹²So then, the Law itself is holy, and the commandment is holy, right, and good. ¹³Does this mean that what is good brought about my death? By no means! It was sin that did it; by using what is good, sin brought death to me in order that its true nature as sin might be revealed. And so, by means of the commandment, sin is shown to be even more terribly sinful.

The Conflict in Man

¹⁴We know that the Law is spiritual; but I am mortal man, sold as a slave to sin. ¹⁵I do not understand what I do; for I don't do what I would like to do, but instead I do what I hate. ¹⁶When I do what I don't want to do, this shows that I agree that the Law is right. ¹⁷So I am not really the one who does this thing; rather it is the sin that lives in me. ¹⁸I know that good does not live in me —that is, in my human nature. For even though the desire to do good is in me, I am not able to do it. ¹⁹I don't do the good I want to do; instead, I do the evil that I do not want to do. ²⁰If I do what I don't want to do, this means that no longer am I the one who does it; instead, it is the sin that lives in me.

²¹So I find that this law is at work: when I want to do what is good, what is evil is the only choice I have. ²²My inner being delights in the law of God. ²³But I see a different law at work in my body—a law that fights against the law that my mind approves of. It makes me a prisoner to the law of sin which is at work in my body. ²⁴What an unhappy man I am! Who will rescue me from this body that is taking me to death? ²⁵Thanks be to God, through our Lord Jesus Christ!

This, then, is my condition: by myself I can serve God's law only with my mind, while my human nature serves the law of sin.

Life in the Spirit

8 There is no condemnation now for those who live in union with Christ Jesus. [2]For the law of the Spirit, which brings us life in union with Christ Jesus, has set me free from the law of sin and death. [3]What the Law could not do, because human nature was weak, God did. He condemned sin in human nature by sending his own Son, who came with a nature like man's sinful nature to do away with sin. [4]God did this so that the righteous demands of the Law might be fully satisfied in us who live according to the Spirit, not according to human nature. [5]Those who live as their human nature tells them to, have their minds controlled by what human nature wants. Those who live as the Spirit tells them to, have their minds controlled by what the Spirit wants. [6]To have your mind controlled by human nature results in death; to have your mind controlled by the Spirit results in life and peace. [7]And so a man becomes an enemy of God when his mind is controlled by human nature; for he does not obey God's law, and in fact he cannot obey it. [8]Those who obey their human nature cannot please God.

[9]But you do not live as your human nature tells you to; you live as the Spirit tells you to—if, in fact, God's Spirit lives in you. Whoever does not have the Spirit of Christ does not belong to him. [10]But if Christ lives in you, although your bodies are going to die because of sin, yet the Spirit is life for you because you have been put right with God. [11]If the Spirit of God, who raised Jesus from death, lives in you, then he who raised Christ from death will also give life to your mortal bodies by the presence of his Spirit in you.

[12]So then, my brothers, we have an obligation, but not to live as our human nature wants us to. [13]For if you live according to your human nature, you are going to die; but if, by the Spirit, you kill your sinful actions, you will live. [14]Those who are led by God's Spirit are God's sons. [15]For the Spirit that God has given you does not make you a slave and cause you to be afraid; instead, the Spirit makes you God's sons, and by the Spirit's power we cry to God, "Father! my

Father!" [16]God's Spirit joins himself to our spirits to declare that we are God's children. [17]Since we are his children, we will possess the blessings he keeps for his people, and we will also possess with Christ what God has kept for him; for if we share Christ's suffering, we will also share his glory.·

The Future Glory

[18]I consider that what we suffer at this present time cannot be compared at all with the glory that is going to be revealed to us. [19]All of creation waits with eager longing for God to reveal his sons. [20]For creation was condemned to become worthless, not of its own will, but because God willed it to be so. Yet there was this hope, [21]that creation itself would one day be set free from its slavery to decay, and share the glorious freedom of the children of God. [22]For we know that up to the present time all of creation groans with pain like the pain of childbirth. [23]But not just creation alone; we who have the Spirit as the first of God's gifts, we also groan within ourselves as we wait for God to make us his sons and set our whole being free. [24]For it was by hope that we were saved; but if we see what we hope for, then it is not really hope. For who hopes for something that he sees? [25]But if we hope for what we do not see, we wait for it with patience.

[26]In the same way the Spirit also comes to help us, weak that we are. For we do not know how we ought to pray; the Spirit himself pleads with God for us, in groans that words cannot express. [27]And God, who sees into the hearts of men, knows what the thought of the Spirit is; because the Spirit pleads with God on behalf of his people and in accordance with his will.

[28]We know that in all things God works for good with those who love him, those whom he has called according to his purpose. [29]Those whom God had already chosen he had also set apart to become like his Son, so that the Son would be the first among many brothers. [30]And so God called those that he had set apart; and those that he called he also put right with

himself; and with those that he put right with himself he also shared his glory.

God's Love in Christ Jesus

[31]Faced with all this, what can we say? If God is for us, who can be against us? [32]He did not even keep back his own Son, but offered him for us all! He gave us his Son—will he not also freely give us all things? [33]Who will accuse God's chosen people? God himself declares them not guilty! [34]Can anyone, then, condemn them? Christ Jesus is the one who died, or rather, who was raised to life and is at the right side of God. He pleads with God for us! [35]Who, then, can separate us from the love of Christ? Can trouble do it, or hardship, or persecution, or hunger, or poverty, or danger, or death? [36]As the scripture says,

> "For your sake we are in danger of death
> the whole day long;
> we are treated like sheep that are going
> to be slaughtered."

[37]No, in all these things we have complete victory through him who loved us! [38]For I am certain that nothing can separate us from his love: neither death nor life;

Nothing can separate us from his love

neither angels nor other heavenly rulers or powers; neither the present nor the future; [39]neither the world above nor the world below—there is nothing in all creation that will ever be able to separate us from the love of God which is ours through Christ Jesus our Lord.

Section 4: God's Power Overcomes Human Weakness

Romans 5:12-8:39

In every age, people have tried to express their experience of evil and to understand it. Some have seen it as a personal power fighting against God with the support of a whole range of lesser evil forces, like a dark army led by a ruthless general. When Christians have used this kind of language they have always been careful to show that God is more powerful than any of the forces which might try to oppose him, even when God's victory may seem to be delayed.

Others see evil as something like the difficulty a carver has when he has to use a particularly hard or twisted piece of wood. It seems to resist him as he tries to shape it and impose his ideas on it, and if it has a knot or a flaw in it his work may be ruined. Some people think that the human body is like this, a hindrance to the soul of man as he tries to put his good intentions into practice.

No Christian can really take a view like this very seriously, even though such great thinkers as Plato have believed it. God made everything there is, including the material universe, and he is not limited by his own creation. To compare God with a craftsman or an artist may be helpful, but there comes a point when the comparison breaks down.

The sense of evil has been conveyed vividly by many authors. One of the most recent and successful was J. R. R. Tolkien in *The Lord of the Rings*, where the main character struggles to rid his world of a force so powerful that it corrupts everyone who has the opportunity of using it. We have had plenty of opportunity to see what power can do to the people who possess it. In the end it seems to possess and control them, and turn everything they plan into something evil.

God is certainly more powerful than anything which may try to drag people away from him, or prevent them from returning to him. But there is nothing automatic about the way in which his power works. He has chosen the way of love, and this requires a response from the beloved if it is to be effective. This is where the resistance is felt. The love of God is there all right, in all its power, but there always seems to be something which stands in the way of returning his love.

Paul felt this acutely, but he also found the solution. There is more to God's love than there ever can be in human love. For God not only begins the loving, he also acts to make it possible for people to respond to him, and he amplifies their response until it matches his own love. God's love lifts people to his own level, if they will allow him to do so. The Holy Spirit leads people to God, and shares with them the innermost privileges of the life of God. They become sons of God, as Jesus is Son of God. Their salvation is far more than an escape from evil. It is a whole new life of utter fulfilment in the closest possible relationship with God.

It is not surprising that Paul found himself over-whelmed by the very thought of it all. This is the destiny not only of mankind but of the whole universe as well. It is as if the cosmos was holding its breath, as it waits to share in the love of God. As man is caught up into his destiny of love, he takes with him the whole creation, of which he is the climax. All things find their meaning in man's response to God's love.

This section of Paul's letter ends with a great shout of confidence and security. God's love is supreme. Nothing at all can possibly separate us from the love which God has made available to us through his Son.

Adam and Christ 5:12-21

Adam and Eve, and the story of their disobedience, seem to create more problems for people than any other part of the Bible. Perhaps it is because they come at the very beginning of the Old Testament, and were so often taught in school as if they were historical people.

The Hebrew story-tellers who first delighted their audiences with the story of Adam and Eve were conveying deep truths about human nature, but they were not reporting history. We can take the truth in the story and let the history go. In this case, if we confuse the truth with the way of pointing to it we shall miss the point.

The point is man's responsibilities, and the chaos he causes when he fails. Man's place in creation is like that of a governor in a province of an empire (to use an unfashionable image), or like the managing director of a great industrial concern. He has great authority, but it is not his own. It is an authority which has been given to him, and he must be loyal to the emperor he represents, or to the board of directors which has appointed him. The emperor, the central government, or the board decide what the fundamental policy shall be. Their representative puts the policy into effect, and maintains it throughout the province or the factory. He is an organizer and a guardian, not a dictator or even a sovereign.

This is what the ancient authors of the book of Genesis meant when they said that man had been made 'in the image of God'. Through man, God's values were to be mediated to the whole of the creation. All things were to find their place in God's love, under man's control.

Such a scheme could only work if man remained loyal to God – and the way of love carried with it the risk that the freedom of love would be abused. If the governor rebelled, or the managing director organized the whole enterprise for his own selfish ends, everything would go wrong. So the story-tellers traced the pain and confusion which flowed from Adam's disobedience.

'The knowledge of good and evil' was far more than mere knowledge, it was control. Man thought that he could decide what was to be good and what was to be condemned in the creation, as it suited his own personal convenience and comfort. Might became right, and God's values were pushed into the background. It was a formula for death and ruin.

Paul was a man of his time, and no doubt he believed in the historical existence of Adam. But he uses the Adam story to point to the wonderful love which God has shown in his Son Jesus Christ. The remedy is far more impressive than the disorder it cures, and far more powerful than the forces of disruption. It is the personal love of God, come into the world from outside, untouched by any trace of weakness or compromise. The love which had brought the world into existence was once more at work in it.

Moral rules and laws, no matter how perfect they might be, could not put things right. They could only show how far things had gone wrong and measure the distance man had moved away from God. It had to be the source of life himself who brought man back to the life God had planned for him, and restored him to dignity. For this is a further wonder about God's salvation.

By man's standards, the rebellious cause of all the misery should have been destroyed, but God gives those who are saved a share in his own rule of the universe. They are restored to their original place and given their true responsibilities. But this time their rule will be 'through Christ'. Once they have allowed themselves to be taken into God's love through Christ, they will be able to face their responsibilities with a new confidence. The new life they share has been shown to be stronger than death itself.

Dead to Sin but Alive in Christ 6:1-14

We are all of us expert in using gestures and interpreting them. They are the symbols by which we communicate with each other. I smile as my wife passes me a cup of tea at breakfast, and kiss her as I leave for work. With frowns and shrugs and nods, raised hats and shaken hands, we supplement the words we use to each other. They are the outward signs which point to our deeper intentions and meanings. They express our relationships with each other.

Baptism is just a sign, symbolizing and expressing a relationship which God has established with us. And at the same time it indicates our response to his saving friendship.

In our own times, when most of us are baptized at so early an age that we cannot possibly remember it, baptism must lose some of its impressiveness. If it is a way of showing our acceptance of God's love, then others must make the response on our behalf, until we are old enough to accept our privileges and responsibilities for ourselves. Only when we are older will we realize our need for spiritual washing, and appreciate the new life in God which grows from it.

That new life is symbolized in another way by baptism, and here again the modern custom of merely pouring a little water over a person's head weakens the symbolism. For the first Christians, baptism was a real descent into the water. As the newly baptized climbed the steps again, and were given new clothes to wear, they acted out their emergence into their new life.

Like Christ, they had passed through death, and now they had put their old life behind them. Whatever the world might think, they had turned their backs on the imperfection and wickedness of life lived without God. They were sharing in Christ's risen life, and belonged no more to the world where death reigns supreme.

We sometimes talk as if symbols and the actions which show how we feel belong to an outmoded and old-fashioned way of life. They are fine for children, who enjoy play-acting, or for a simpler age. Nothing could be farther from the truth. As we accept an ever more complex way of living, and command ever more sophisticated technological advances, we need more than ever the actions which remind us of our real needs.

Without God we are failures who create death and misery, and we are dragged down into the mess that we have made. We have learned to manipulate the things that God has made, even to manipulate other people. But we bring nothing really new into existence. All that is good and true and enduring comes from God. When we are new-made, we can begin to see things as they really are, and surrender ourselves to the love which God pours into us.

Such a cleansing from the past, and a renewal for the future, opens up entirely different opportunities and responsibilities. We have been transformed. We can experience a freedom like blind people who have been given sight, or cripples who find that they can run. In their old life they only longed to be freed from their limitations and restrictions. Only when they are freed do they begin to realize the vast new possibilities that are opening out before them.

Slaves of Righteousness 6:15-23

Christ's victory over evil opened up a new way of approaching God. We are all accustomed to regulating our lives by rules and laws, even in the most ordinary matters. As a driver, I know that a whole host of laws apply to me and my car, from the moment I buy it until it is finally scrapped, and no matter how I use it. It may well be that in a perfect world, populated by perfect people, none of those laws would be needed. There would be no need to restrict speed in a built-up area, for everyone would drive at a safe speed, and no need to define right of way at roundabouts, for everyone would drive with full consideration for other people on the road. The argument becomes stronger for more serious matters, such as murder or deliberate fraud.

Yet we all know of situations where laws are not needed. A really close friendship, or a marriage lived out in the deepest love, are not regulated by laws. The people involved express their relationship with each other with a freedom which no laws could ever define. They have no need of law.

It would be unthinkable to suppose that Christ's relationship with the Father is controlled by law; it is a union of perfect love. This is what Christ has opened to us, the chance of sharing in the utterly free and spontaneous love through which God expresses himself. It is the key to our links with each other, as well as our links with God. Once we enter into this kind of life, we pass beyond any need of law. We are free.

Insights like this must have made people say that Paul thought sin did not matter. Christians are 'above the law' and can sin as much as they like! Paul corrects this crude travesty of Christian freedom with a daring comparison drawn from slavery. It was the common background for all people of his time, so everyone would appreciate his point.

The new life in Christ is like a change of masters, but it is a change from a ruthless and harsh task master to one whose sole concern is for the welfare and happiness of the people in his charge. The first imposes his rule by force, the second by a love which produces a free response of love. Both can be seen as a kind of surrender, but the first is against the will of the subjugated slave, the second confers freedom and respect. In fact, it raises man to the level of God himself as he grows into the measure of God's love.

Modern comparisons are not easy, but perhaps the difference between a partner in a business and an exploited employee comes close to it. The partner may well give far more time and energy to his work, for less money, than the disgruntled employee who feels that he has no say in what he is doing. But the closest comparisons must be in the realms of marriage and friendship, for if there is any trace of exploitation or oppression in them the whole relationship is soured. The free interchange of love is real freedom, no matter how restricting it may seem to those who have no experience of it.

An Illustration from Marriage 7:1-6

The change of attitude brought about by Christianity, when its teaching is taken seriously, cuts across all human conventions. The change of attitude, says Paul, is as thorough as the change brought about by death, and as complete. To illustrate his point, Paul reminds his readers about the laws controlling marriage in Jewish society. The wife is tied to her husband with bonds which she can do nothing to break. If she goes with another man, she commits adultery and must suffer the penalty for it.

But once her husband dies, she is free to do whatever she wishes. If she marries again she is doing nothing wrong. Death has severed her old obligations, and she can enter into a new life.

In a strange way, this is what Jesus has done for mankind. The old way of life, which rejected, condemned and killed him, lies in the past. The old bonds have been broken, and Jesus has passed through the death barrier into the new life which lies the other side of it.

In fact, he showed that new life in everything he did, even before his death. The power of undefeatable love was at work and was shown to everyone he met, if only they were willing to recognize it. The forces of rejection and death were wasting their time when they tried to kill him. They only demonstrated how strong God's love really is.

'You are part of the body of Christ', writes Paul. To catch the full force of what he is saying, it is necessary to read what he had already written in 1 Corinthians 12. He will pick up this same theme again in this present letter (Romans 12), for it is one of the most fundamental beliefs the first Christians had about their relationship with Jesus.

They could use God's love because they were sharing in Christ's power of love. They could cope with all the stresses and strains of life in the world because Jesus had already experienced all the suffering that life can bring, and had shown that it could not defeat him. Indeed, the stresses only show Christians how fully they are already sharing in Christ's risen life. They are free at last from the restrictions and limitations of their past.

As civilization develops and life becomes more complex, so the problems of living multiply. We know, nowadays, how thoroughly entangled the affairs of a nation can get, and the problems of the individual people who form it. We are dependent on each other on a worldwide scale, and the results can be catastrophic as nations jockey for advantage. No system of law can even express the complication of human relationships, let alone control the damage of selfish or mistaken decisions. God offers another kind of solution. His love is available in all its proved effectiveness. It transcends all the complications, and the failure of law.

Law and Sin 7:7-13

One of the first of the prophets to try to get the Hebrew people to see sense was a shepherd, Amos. He spoke his mind during a period of prosperity and complacency. In terms of economic growth, the nation was doing well. Trade was flooding along the great international routes which passed through Palestine; the property developers were transforming the towns; surplus wealth was supporting a luxury market for skilled jewellers and carvers of ivory.

The weak went to the wall: the poor, the landless, aliens, orphans, widows. Even in the courts, the wealthy bought the decisions. Religion flourished, but it had very little to do with life; in fact, it only increased the people's complacency. They felt that nothing could go wrong so long as the sacrifices were offered and the ritual performed properly.

Amos spoke against it all in vain, and the people only listened to him when he was denouncing the wickedness of their traditional enemies. Even the appeal to the past was ineffective, when God had rescued them from degradation and slavery in Egypt. They should have remembered that God would not tolerate any of his people being treated with contempt; the degraded, the weak and the poor had a special claim to protection.

At last, Amos made his point with a builder's plumbline, the simple level which a bricklayer uses to make sure that the wall is not leaning to one side or the other. If the bob of lead swings out of its hole, the wall must be pulled down and rebuilt. (See Amos 7:7-9.)

The Law, says Paul, is a true standard of God's goodness, but it only produces the condemnation of man. Compared with that absolute standard, man must find himself out of true. If the standard had never been known, man's sinfulness would have gone undetected, so his condemnation is the result of law. But the Law has not caused the sin, it has only shown it up.

The point is important, for Paul could be accused of despising the religion he had left, and rejecting two thousand years of Jewish religious experience. If Paul is exposed to such criticism, it can certainly be levelled against later Christians who so easily condemn or underrate Judaism and other faiths. The long centuries of Christian persecution of Jews is sad evidence. Paul can be acquitted of this charge. His only complaint against the Jewish religious law is its ineffectiveness. It shows what is wrong but has no power to put it right.

Human nature being what it is, there is even a pleasure in defying the Law, perhaps out of a perverse sense of independence. The rebellious schoolboy may well be asserting his dignity and his individuality when he defies the school rules. He needs personal recognition of his value, rather than condemnation. He needs something which will turn his efforts into positive achievements, because the very qualities which lead him into trouble can be the assets by which he grows to full maturity. It is what God does for rebellious man, through Christ.

The Two Natures in Man 7:14-25

With this section we reach one of the most revealing passages in any of Paul's letters, in which he shows that he knows to the full how difficult the way of Christ can be.

An important key to this section is the way in which Paul uses the word 'law'. He is thinking of law in the way that a scientist uses it, rather than the meaning a lawyer gives to it or a policeman. Law, for Paul, means a pattern of behaviour, or the shape taken by a series of events. The life of a criminal can have a consistency about it, even though it breaks all the 'laws' in the legal sense, and then you can say that his actions follow a law of their own. So Paul can talk about 'the law of God' and 'the law of sin'. In the next section he will find another pattern, another way of life, 'the law of the Spirit'. He is like a scientist examining a complicated situation, and identifying the patterns in it.

When Paul examines his own behaviour, the main pattern he discovers there is an evil one. He knows perfectly well what would be the right thing to do, and he wants to do it, but the only choice he seems to make is an evil one. He is drawn towards the very course of action which his mind and his conscience reject. He has lost control and he feels that he is in the grip of an alien force.

The knowledge of the good way is of no use to him when he experiences this power of evil. It can only tell him that he is going wrong; there is nothing this 'law of God' seems able to do to prevent him from going wrong. If this seems a strange experience, we can recognize it whenever we are tempted to say to some child, 'You knew perfectly well that it was wrong, so why did you do it?'

Knowing what is right is not enough. God must do more than set us a good example, or teach us the right way. He must give us the power to put his teaching into practice and follow his example, if we are to be saved from 'the law of sin' which dominates us. Without God's power, man is helpless to break from his old ways.

In recent times the full horror of drug addiction has dawned on the western world. People in its grip know full well that it is ruining them; they are desperate to be normal again and to be rid of its terrible domination. Even when they receive medical help, they experience appalling withdrawal symptoms. The return to normality is a long, slow process during which they need all the external help they can get. Breaking with sin is something like this. 'Who will rescue me?' asks Paul.

He finds the answer in Jesus Christ. The human need points to something more than an expert teacher or a perfect example, when it finds the answer to all its problems in Christ. Christ turns good intentions into facts, and shares with man his own power to put his teaching into practice and to follow his example. If he did not do that, Christ would be the supreme frustration for man, showing him an ideal which he could not reach. But we need not fear, for God has provided the means to perfection along with the perfection he promised for us.

Life in the Spirit 8:1-17

There is a third 'law', a third way of life available, which sets us free from our helplessness. 'The law of the Spirit' gives us the power to resist the evil way and to become like Christ. Our efforts are no longer thwarted, and the example shown to us by Jesus has not been in vain.

Knowing that we have the help of the Holy Spirit can change our whole outlook. The timid climber is filled with confidence when he is roped to an expert who has made that climb before. A spate of people break the four-minute mile barrier once it has been done by one supreme athlete. Every member of an operating team becomes more dependable when the team is led by an outstandingly able surgeon.

All comparisons such as these fade when they are compared with the effects of God's Spirit as he comes to man's aid. All possibilities are transformed. This was the power by which Jesus lived, the point of view which he brought to the problems of human existence and personal relationships. He was successful as no one had ever been, and retained his consistent power to love to the point of death and beyond it. Nothing on earth could overwhelm him, or make him betray the way of life which he taught to others. 'You must be perfect,' he said, 'just as your Father in heaven is perfect.' By the power of the Spirit, Jesus showed what this meant, and rose from death to demonstrate that there is no limit to what God can do.

There is no real point in trying to sort out whether it is the Father, the Son or the Spirit who is at work here. God himself is a community of love who is beyond all merely human reasoning and logic. In the same breath, Paul writes that Christ lives in us, the Spirit lives in us, and he 'who raised Jesus from death' will give life to us. The salvation which God offers is entry into the most intimate life of God, to share in the love which is the very being of God.

To describe this, Paul draws on the experience of life within a family. No matter how exalted the parents may be, the children can address them with familiar ease and in a specially intimate language. This is the privilege conferred on us by the Spirit – we become sons of God just as Jesus has always been Son of God. We can address God as Father in the most familiar way, for it is worth noticing that Paul uses the local diminutive with which a Jewish child would address his father. 'Daddy' would be nearer the mark.

It is a striking example to use to describe the wonders of God's salvation, especially when we remember that Paul is using it for a society which took a harsh and cruel world for granted. There is nothing artificial or incomplete about the love which God gives to those who will accept it, for it takes them into the final security of belonging fully to the family of God.

The human spirit is not overwhelmed or suppressed by the presence of God; quite the opposite. It is like a mother teaching a baby to walk. She supports him as he totters along. Only a fraction of the total effort can come from the child, but the mother amplifies it so that he can move with confidence. Some time in the future he will grow to be a man, and will be able to do for himself what he could at one time only achieve with the help of others.

Our puny efforts to live as God's children have to be amplified if they are to be of any use, but this small beginning will develop into full personal response to God's love, so that we can love as we are loved. Then we shall have come to the perfection for which we have been made, and share to the full in the glory of Christ.

The Future Glory 8:18-30

Since the war of 1939-45, there has been a spate of escape stories. The cinema, television, colour supplements and books in their hundreds have all presented us with accounts of people struggling to be free. Even the most carefully guarded fortresses, hundreds of miles of enemy-controlled country, and strong frontier patrols have not deterred them. The prisoners, or the oppressed, will plan for years, take enormous risks and will patiently accept hardship and suffering for the sake of the new life of freedom which lies at the end of their journey.

The salvation which God offers us has something of this quality about it. We are in transit. At the end of the journey lies complete freedom and the fulfilment of all our hopes. Beyond the fortress and the enemy country is a land where we shall be in unhindered communion with God, where our lives will be filled with his love.

There is no need to surrender to the frustration and imperfection of the world in which we live, still less do we have to conform to its standards in order to survive. The decisive victory over evil has already been won by Jesus Christ, and it is now only a matter of making his rule effective throughout his kingdom.

All human comparisons fall down in the end. Nothing can really describe what God has done and the glory he has made available. For once, it is not too good to be true. Hopes and ideals are fulfilled in a perfection far beyond anything we can imagine.

The plan embraces the entire universe, rather than just the human part of it. Man is as much part of the world as are the animals, plants and the natural resources which he feels he can exploit as he wishes. All is one whole in which the various parts all depend on each other. It is a single community.

This is a view which great thinkers have struggled to express from the earliest times to our own day, from Aristotle to Teilhard de Chardin, and from ancient Buddhism to the philosophy which lies at the heart of Marxism.

The details of such systems of thought may be unacceptable to Christianity or to particular groups of Christians, but there is a truth at the heart of them all. None of us are solitary, independent, self-sufficient creatures. Nor is mankind as a whole. We have a common destiny, just as we have a common need, along with the whole of creation.

Meanwhile, we are living in an interim period, and it is bound to cause us suffering. In a way, the suffering is a result of the love which we share with God. If Jesus had not loved, he would not have met with such opposition; he could have compromised and conformed to the standards of the people of his time. But he lived by the perfect love of God, and those who would not accept its standards hated it. We suffer even as we grow closer to the glory, and we know how weak we are as we draw closer to the strength which sustains the whole creation.

This is where the Spirit comes into his own, for we are not thrown back on our own unaided efforts as we struggle to respond to God's love and to express it in our lives. Our efforts and our response are amplified by the Spirit and made part of his creative power. We already experience something of the facility to love and to succeed which ultimately will be ours to the full.

It may seem a strange way of going about it. It is the only way which respects our freedom and our capacity to act responsibly. If we were fit for nothing better than slavery, our salvation would be forced on us and we would have no contribution to make to it. God's way is the way of love. The journey ends in lovers meeting.

God's Love in Jesus Christ 8:31-9

With this section, Paul completes the main part of his letter. He has set out the basic truths of the Christian message of hope and salvation as he has experienced it. This is the gospel – the Good News – for man at any time, as true in the twentieth century as it was in the first.

It is appropriate that Paul should end his main analysis with a description of Christian confidence, for he had only recently been reminded of its real foundations. Paul's work as a Christian in the eastern part of the Roman Empire had brought him more than his share of hardship and suffering, despite his privileged position as a Roman citizen. In 2 Corinthians 11:21-9, the letter he wrote immediately before this one to Rome, he described some of the unpleasant things that had happened to him. Yet he had found that they only increased his confidence.

Earlier in the same letter Paul had told the Corinthians what suffering had taught him and the other apostles. No matter how overwhelming it threatened to be, they found that they came through it safely. The experience of mortal danger only served to show them that they were supremely well protected: 'We are often troubled, but not crushed; sometimes in doubt, but never in despair; there are many enemies, but we are never without a friend; and though badly hurt at times. we are not destroyed . . . Throughout our lives we are always in danger of death for Jesus' sake, in order that his life may be seen in this mortal body of ours.' (2 Corinthians 4:8-11)

Nothing can separate us from the love of God. Our own experience can prove this to us. But there is a greater proof available, in the life, death and resurrection of Jesus. However nonsensical the idea may seem, Jesus is God suffering. The rejections, the disappointments, the enmity experienced by Jesus during his life on earth, all coming to their climax in his. condemnation and cruel death, show how far God will go to reach man. He remains faithful in the face of all setbacks. Nothing will stop God's love. Nothing can separate us from it.

Whatever forces in our world – or in ourselves – may seem to stand between us and God, they are all inferior to the power of his love. When God raised Jesus from death, he showed where the real power lay. That power was at work in every moment of Jesus' life, and in everything he did or said. It was his glory. And we are already sharing in it.

ROMANS 9:1-11:36

God and His Chosen People

9 What I say is true; I belong to Christ and I do not lie. My conscience, ruled by the Holy Spirit, also assures me that I am not lying. ²How great is my sorrow, how endless the pain in my heart for my people, my own flesh and blood! ³For their sake I could wish that I myself were under God's curse and separated from Christ. ⁴They are God's chosen people; he made them his sons and shared his glory with them; he made his covenants with them and gave them the Law; they have the true worship; they have received God's promises; ⁵they are descended from the patriarchs, and Christ, as a human being, belongs to their race. May God, who rules over all, be praised forever! Amen.

⁶I am not saying that the promise of God has failed; because not all the people of Israel are the chosen people of God. ⁷Neither are all Abraham's descendants the children of God. God said to Abraham, "The descendants of Isaac will be counted as yours." ⁸This means that the children born in the natural way are not the children of God; instead, the children born as a result of God's promise are regarded as the true descendants. ⁹For God's promise was made in these words: "At the right time I will come back and Sarah will have a son."

¹⁰And this is not all. For Rebecca's two sons had the same father, our ancestor Isaac. ¹¹⁻¹²But in order that the choice of one son might be completely the result of God's own purpose, God said to her, "The older will serve the younger." He said this before they were born, before they had done anything either good or bad; so God's choice was based on his call, and not on anything they did. ¹³As the scripture says, "I loved Jacob, but I hated Esau."

¹⁴What shall we say, then? That God is unjust? Not at all. ¹⁵For he said to Moses, "I will have mercy on whom I wish, I will take pity on whom I wish." ¹⁶So then, it does not depend on what man wants or does, but only on God's mercy. ¹⁷For the scripture says to Pharaoh, "I made you king for this very purpose, to use you to show my power, and to make my name known in all the world." ¹⁸So then, God has mercy on whom he wishes, and he makes stubborn whom he wishes.

God's Wrath and Mercy

¹⁹One of you, then, will say to me, "If this is so, how can God find fault with a man? Who can resist God's will?" ²⁰But who are you, my friend, to talk back to God? A clay pot does not ask the man who made it, "Why did you make me like this?" ²¹After all, the man who makes the pots has the right to use the clay as he wishes, and to make two pots from the same lump of clay, one for special occasions, and the other for ordinary use.

²²And the same is true of what God has done. He wanted to show his wrath and to make his power known.

So he was very patient in enduring those who were the objects of his wrath, who were ready to be destroyed. [23]And he wanted also to reveal his rich glory, which was poured out on us who are the objects of his mercy, those of us whom he has prepared to receive his glory. [24]For we are the ones whom he called, not only from among the Jews but also from among the Gentiles. [25]This is what he says in the book of Hosea,

> "The people who were not mine,
> I will call 'My People.'
> The nation that I did not love,
> I will call 'My Beloved.'
> [26] And in the very place where they were
>   told, 'You are not my people,'
>   there they will be called the sons of the
>   living God."

[27]And Isaiah exclaims about Israel, "Even if the people of Israel are as many as the grains of sand by the sea, yet only a few of them will be saved; [28]for the Lord will quickly settle his full account with all the world." [29]It is as Isaiah had said before, "If the Lord Almighty had not left us some descendants, we would have become like Sodom, we would have been like Gomorrah."

Israel and the Gospel

[30]What shall we say, then? This: that the Gentiles, who were not trying to put themselves right with God, were put right with him through faith; [31]while the chosen people, who were seeking a law that would put them right with God, did not find it. [32]And why not? Because what they did was not based on faith but on works. They stumbled over the "stumbling stone" [33]that the scripture speaks of:

> "Look, I place in Zion a stone
>   that will make people stumble,
>   a rock that will make them fall.
> But whoever believes in him will not be
>   disappointed."

10 My brothers, how I wish with all my heart that my own people might be saved! How I pray to God for them! [2]I can be a witness for them that they are deeply devoted to God. But their devotion is not based on true knowledge. [3]They have not known the way in

which God puts men right with himself, and have tried to set up their own way; and so they did not submit themselves to God's way of putting men right. [4]For Christ has brought the Law to an end, so that everyone who believes is put right with God.

Salvation Is for All

[5]This is what Moses wrote about being put right with God by obeying the Law: "Whoever does what the Law commands will live by it." [6]But this is what is said about being put right with God through faith: "Do not say to yourself, Who will go up into heaven?" (that is, to bring Christ down). [7]"Do not say either, Who will go down into the world below?" (that is, to bring Christ up from the dead). [8]What it says is this: "God's message is near you, on your lips and in your heart"—that is, the message of faith that we preach. [9]If you declare with your lips, "Jesus is Lord," and believe in your heart that God raised him from the dead, you will be saved. [10]For we believe in our hearts and are put right with God; we declare with our lips and are saved. [11]The scripture says, "Whoever believes in him will not be disappointed." [12]This includes everyone, because there is no difference between Jews and Gentiles; God is the same Lord of all, and richly blesses all who call to him. [13]As the scripture says, "Everyone who calls on the name of the Lord will be saved."

[14]But how can they call to him, if they have not believed? And how can they believe, if they have not heard the message? And how can they hear, if the message is not proclaimed? [15]And how can the message be proclaimed, if the messengers are not sent out? As the scripture says, "How wonderful is the coming of those who bring good news!" [16]But they have not all accepted the Good News. Isaiah himself said, "Lord, who believed our message?" [17]So then, faith comes from hearing the message, and the message comes through preaching Christ.

[18]But I ask: Is it true that they did not hear the message? Of course they did—as the scripture says:

> "The sound of their voices went out to
>   all the world;

their words reached the ends of the
    earth."

[19]Again I ask: Did the people of Israel not know? Moses
himself is the first one to answer:

"I will make you jealous of a people who
    are not a real nation;
I will make you angry with a nation of
    foolish people."

[20]And Isaiah is bolder when he says,

"I was found by those who were not
    looking for me,
I appeared to those who were not
    asking for me."

[21]But concerning Israel he says, "I held out my hands
the whole day long to a disobedient and rebellious people."

God's Mercy on Israel

11 I ask, then: Did God reject his own people? Certainly not! I myself am an Israelite, a descendant
of Abraham, a member of the tribe of Benjamin. [2]God
has not rejected his people, whom he chose from the
beginning. You know what the scripture says in the
passage where Elijah pleads with God against Israel:
[3]"Lord, they have killed your prophets and torn down
your altars; I am the only one left, and they are trying
to kill me." [4]What answer did God give him? "I have
kept for myself seven thousand men who have not worshipped the false god Baal." [5]It is the same way now at
this time: there is a small number of those whom God
has chosen, because of his mercy. [6]His choice is based
on his mercy, not on what they have done. For if God's
choice were based on what men do, then his mercy
would not be true mercy.

[7]What then? The people of Israel did not find what
they were looking for. It was the small group that God
chose who found it; the rest grew deaf to God's call. [8]As
the scripture says, "God made them dull of heart and
mind; to this very day they cannot see with their eyes
or hear with their ears." [9]And David says,

"May they be caught and trapped at
    their feasts;
may they fall, may they be punished!

¹⁰ May their eyes be closed so that they
cannot see;
and make them bend under their
troubles at all times."

¹¹I ask, then: When the Jews stumbled, did they fall
to their ruin? By no means! Because they sinned, salvation has come to the Gentiles, to make the Jews jealous
of them. ¹²The sin of the Jews brought rich blessings to
the world, and their spiritual poverty brought rich blessings to the Gentiles. How much greater the blessings
will be, then, when the complete number of Jews is
included!

The Salvation of the Gentiles

¹³I am speaking now to you Gentiles: as long as I am
an apostle to the Gentiles I will take pride in my work.
¹⁴Perhaps I can make the people of my own race jealous,
and so be able to save some of them. ¹⁵For when they
were rejected, the world was made friends with God.
What will it be, then, when they are accepted? It will be
life for the dead!

A wild olive tree has been joined to it

¹⁶If the first piece of bread is given to God, then the
whole loaf is his also; and if the roots of a tree are offered
to God, the branches are his also. ¹⁷Some of the
branches of the cultivated olive tree have been broken
off, and the branch of a wild olive tree has been joined
to it. You Gentiles are like that wild olive tree, and now

you share the strength and rich life of the Jews. [18]So then, you must not despise those who were broken off like branches. How can you be proud? You are just a branch; you don't support the root—the root supports you.

[19]But you will say, "Yes, but the branches were broken off to make room for me." [20]This is true. They were broken off because they did not believe, while you remain in place because you believe. But do not have proud thoughts about it; instead, be afraid. [21]God did not spare the Jews, who are like natural branches; do you think he will spare you? [22]Here we see how kind and how severe God is. He is severe towards those who have fallen, but kind to you—if you continue in his kindness; but if you do not, you too will be broken off. [23]And the Jews, if they abandon their unbelief, will be put back in the place where they were, because God is able to put them back again. [24]You Gentiles are like the branch of a wild olive tree that is broken off, and then, contrary to nature, is joined to the cultivated olive tree. The Jews are like this cultivated tree; and it will be much easier, then, for God to join these broken-off branches back to their own tree.

God's Mercy on All

[25]There is a secret truth, my brothers, which I want you to know. It will keep you from thinking how wise you are. It is this: the stubbornness of the people of Israel is not permanent, but will last only until the complete number of Gentiles comes to God. [26]And this is how all Israel will be saved. As the scripture says,

"The Saviour will come from Zion,
    and remove all wickedness from the descendants of Jacob.
[27] I will make this covenant with them,
    when I take away their sins."

[28]Because they reject the Good News, the Jews are God's enemies for the sake of you, the Gentiles. But because of God's choice, they are his friends for the sake of the patriarchs. [29]For God does not change his mind about whom he chooses and blesses. [30]As for you Gentiles, you disobeyed God in the past; but now you have

received God's mercy because the Jews disobeyed. ³¹In the same way, because of the mercy that you have received, the Jews now disobey God, in order that they also may now receive God's mercy. ³²For God has made all men prisoners of disobedience, that he might show mercy to them all.

Praise to God

³³How great are God's riches! How deep are his wisdom and knowledge! Who can explain his decisions? Who can understand his ways? ³⁴As the scripture says,
"Who knows the mind of the Lord?
Who is able to give him advice?
³⁵ Who has ever given him anything,
so that he had to pay it back?"
³⁶For all things were created by him, and all things exist through him and for him. To God be the glory forever! Amen.

Section 5: God's Plan: Jews and Gentiles
Romans 9:1-11:36

The three chapters which form this section of Paul's letter are entirely taken up with the Jewish question. If ever a question remained unsolved after all these years, this is it. The twentieth century has seen history's most thorough and terrible attempt to exterminate the Jews, in the concentration camps of Europe. And it has also seen the first successful revival since biblical times of an independent Jewish state, only to find that the same old problems raise their heads again.

Wherever our loyalties may lie, no Christian can feel happy about the way that Jews have been treated by Christians down the ages. Even in biblical times, during the thirteen centuries from Moses to Christ, the Jews were only free to govern themselves for three brief periods of time. Their homeland lay across one of the most important international routes in the world, which great powers fought over to protect their trade and their empires.

In the earliest years of Christianity, the Jewish religion

did all it could to stifle the new Christian movement, but in AD 70 Jerusalem itself was destroyed by the Romans in the Jewish-Roman war, and the Jews lost what little political freedom they still possessed as a nation. They were not to regain it until 1948. The Christian persecution of Jews began almost as soon as the Romans accepted Christianity as the official state religion, in the fourth century, and it has continued ever since. No Christian country has been without its pogroms or its strongly supported antisemitism, at some time in its history.

Paul wrestles with the problem in a sympathetic way, and with an acknowledgement of his own personal feelings. He had been brought up in a wealthy Jewish family living in an attractive Greek-type university city, and clearly he had a great affection for the religion of his childhood and youth. His only regret was that his fellow-Jews had not accepted the Christian gospel. It was the fulfilment of all they held dear, the final development of all the most valuable insights of their religion.

There are some stern warnings for non-Jewish Christians in these chapters. Christians could easily develop the same attitudes which had led to the downfall of the Jews. They could think themselves safe and privileged, and become complacent. Their religion could become one of mere outward conformity instead of a response from the heart. If God could reject the ones whom he had first chosen and for whom he had done so much, he would certainly reject the Christians who had stepped into their place if they made the same mistakes.

The solution offered by Paul to the Jewish question is one which sees their exclusion as no more than a temporary condition. Paul cannot believe that they are lost for ever. The time will come when they will return as a nation, and renew their fellowship with God in the new covenant he has made with his world through his Son Jesus. Then there will indeed be rejoicing.

Meanwhile, many Jews, like Paul, have already reached the goal which God had planned for his chosen people from the first. They must remind their fellow-Christians that the Jews are still God's friends for the sake of the promises he made to their ancestors, for God does not change his mind about his friends.

God and His Chosen People 9:1-18

From other letters of Paul's, it is clear that he took great pride in his Jewish ancestry and his early upbringing. Indeed, in a world as corrupt as that of ancient Rome, a Jewish childhood in a devout family must have been as fine a start in life as could be imagined. Add to that one of the most famous of all teachers, Gamaliel, at the great law school in Jerusalem, and the trust of the nation's leaders, and it is easy to understand why Paul felt such nostalgia for the Jewish way of life.

It hurt him deeply to know that his nation had lost its way. They were the people of God, chosen and prepared down the centuries to be a bridgehead for God's love. Their way of life was to be an example to the rest of the world, to show all people how attractive it was to live in God's kingdom. They were to be models of good government and social responsibility, as their worship directed the power of God into every aspect of their lives.

The Jewish sacred scriptures, the Old Testament, describe how the nation was founded in a long series of covenants with God. The first covenant of all had been with Noah, they believed (Genesis 9), to show that God's blessings were for all mankind. But the blessings would reach the world through covenants with the Jewish nation, made with Abraham (Genesis 12), Isaac (Genesis 26:3-4), Jacob (Genesis 28:13-15), and above all Moses (Exodus 19-24).

The covenant was renewed at every major period of Hebrew history, from Joshua, through David, to the Jews who returned from Babylon to rebuild Jerusalem after their exile. For eighteen centuries the Jews had been proud of their special position and their special responsibilities towards God. Although they had been subjected to foreign rule for most of that time, they had always felt free, and they had always been ready to die for their faith.

At the centre of their lives was the sacred Law, which they believed God had given to Moses. More than anything else, it held them together as a people, even when they were scattered right across the civilized world. For more than six centuries before Paul's letter to Rome, there had been more Jews living outside Palestine than in it, yet the Law had kept them together and they had never lost their sense of national identity and destiny. Humanly speaking, Christ himself was a Jew.

Yet they had rejected the Christ, their own Messiah. Above all, they existed to prepare the way for the Messiah, and they had failed to recognize him when he finally came. Now, their place had been taken by the Gentiles. The new people of God were drawn from all nations. There were Jews amongst them, but the Jewish nation was no longer the instrument of God's will.

There is a very important point here, which Paul makes with examples drawn from the Jews' own religious history. God works by a different logic than the one which human beings take for granted, and Paul gives two instances of it.

The first of the Jewish covenants was made with Abraham and with his descendants, but only with one half of his descendants, the line which came through Isaac. The other line, through Ishmael, was not chosen for the special purpose God had in mind. Yet Ishmael was the boy born by natural, normal means, whereas Isaac was only conceived by a special intervention of God. Isaac's mother, Sarah, was barren, and only conceived Isaac as a result of God's promise. The Jews should have learned to expect the unexpected.

Again, whatever human laws may say about the eldest son inheriting the main privileges and responsibilities, God is not bound by human ideas of the best way of doing things. In fact, the younger of Isaac's two sons, Jacob, inherited the leadership of the chosen people, and the authority of the covenant passed through him.

Everything depends, at each stage, on God's initiative and God's choice of the best way. There is nothing automatic about it. Least of all is birth alone enough. There must be active response to God's personal acts of love. John the Baptist had reminded his listeners that God could raise up children of Abraham from the stones lying around (Matthew 3:9); mere physical descent was certainly no guarantee of inheriting God's promises. It was a truth which Paul would apply to his fellow-Christians later in this section of his letter. Christians in any age could easily make the same mistake as the Jews.

God's Wrath and Mercy 9:19-29

How can man be blamed for his state if he is only what God has made of him? It would be a fair question if God had not reached to the depths to meet the needs of every man and woman, to lift them into unimaginable perfection.

A terrible possibility opens up. Perhaps the evil we discover in ourselves, and the evil by which we are surrounded, has been created by God so that he can demonstrate his power. A strong man can only show how strong he is if his strength is tested; patience only shows when there is something to be patient about. God's strength and love would be nothing like so impressive if it were not resisted.

It is a real possibility. God is the absolute ruler of the universe, its creator and its sustainer. By human standards he has the right to do whatever he wants with it. The builder of the house can build it as he wishes, and pull it down again if it does not please him. The potter can make what he wants with the clay.

It would be a reasonable argument if people were pots, but they are not. They have been made capable of love, and we can dare to argue that there is an obligation on God to allow them to love. They cannot be made and unmade at a whim. People cannot be manipulated as if they were mere objects, not even by God.

Paul has used the comparison to emphasize the wonder of God's love. His almighty power is only ever used for good. By any human standard God would have wiped out his universe long ago, and started again. In Paul's world, the most apt comparison would have been a slave-owner whose slaves had rebelled against him. The Roman world knew how to deal with such a situation, and it did so with utter ruthlessness, to show where the power lay.

In the black-and-white world of law, condemnation and destruction would be the only way out of the human situation. But God has opened up another way, and the wonder of it would never be appreciated if the way of human justice was not kept in mind. God's way with sin has been shown in the infinite love of Jesus Christ and the lengths to which he went to make that love available and effective. In Christ, the rich glory of God has been poured out on all men, and continues until they finally accept it.

God's power may be a frightening thing to contemplate, but it is the essential background for our salvation. If God does not take the initiative to save us, we are not saved.

In one of his parables, Jesus told the story of a man who hired workmen for his vineyard (Matthew 20:1-16). Some were hired early in the morning and worked throughout the day; some started at noon and only worked for the afternoon; some were engaged later, and even at the very end of the day. Yet all were paid the same wages, which they had agreed to before they started. Naturally enough, there were complaints from the ones who had worked longest, but they were told that they had received what they were promised.

Even so, that is not the real point. At the end of the parable, Jesus summed it up: 'So those who are last will be first, and those who are first will be last.' God may indeed have acted irrationally by human logic, but he has done so to save those who ought to be nowhere at all, let alone last. He has made them first in his kingdom. And in doing so, he transforms them into people worthy of his glory, so that they can share the stature of his Son. It is power all right, but power exercised for the salvation of the weak, even when they have brought their weakness upon themselves.

Israel and the Gospel 9:30-10:4

Independence is one of the most admired and prized of human possessions. Deep within us there is a deep dislike of being dependent on anyone, of having to work under other people, of being limited by the decisions of our fellow-men. There is something very valuable in this feeling, for it points to responsible action and the essential dignity of human beings. The person who will stand by his decisions, and risk all on his own efforts, is admired. He or she receives the kind of respect that should be paid to all human beings.

This attitude lay at the heart of the Jews in their approach to God. Rightly, they saw that God's choice of them created obligations for them. It was not an unconditional favour, it was selection for a special task, and they recognized this. They were rescued from their slavery for a purpose: 'From this you know that now, if you obey my voice and hold fast to my covenant, you of all the nations shall be my very own for all the earth is mine. I will count you a kingdom of priests, a conse-crated nation.' (Exodus 19:5-6)

They were to symbolize the whole world's response to God's creative love; they were to show what that love is like, in the way they treated each other, and in their treat-ment of other nations.

It was a fine ideal – and it can still serve as a model for Christians. But the Jews reversed it. They reached a stage where they seemed to think that they had been chosen *because* they were faithful to God. They thought that they deserved God's choice, that they had earned it and that they kept it by their own efforts. God had made them right with himself when he rescued them and chose them. They turned this righteousness into self-righteousness, a subtle but fundamental mistake.

Paul has no doubt about the Jews' devotion to God, and who could have any doubts when they see how Jews are prepared to suffer so deeply for the sake of their religion? 'But their devotion is not based on true knowl-edge. They have not known the way in which God puts men right with himself, and have tried to set up their own way . . .' (Romans 10:2-3)

However independent we may wish to be, the fact remains that we are creatures who cannot even exist, let alone do anything right, without complete trust in God. Our own ideas of the best way are bound to go wrong, and even the solutions discovered by previous genera-tions may prove to be wrong for later times. God's way has to be learned for each new situation and each new generation. And we have to know that we are dependent on his love in everything we do.

This is what faith means. There can be no once-for-all summary of the perfect way of life, such as the Law tries to provide. The perfect way of life is a living relationship with God, such as Jesus showed. Those who trust in Jesus as Son of God come in full power, share in his perfect response to God.

All that was good about the Law is summed up in

Jesus, but in a way which makes that good possible for man. Jesus told his disciples, just before his arrest, that he was the way, the truth, and the life (John 14:6); all mankind now had a new and effective link with God, if they would only put their complete trust in Jesus.

Salvation Is for All 10:5-21

At the centre of the Christian gospel is the message that mankind is no longer dependent on external means of reaching God. Laws, teachers, organizations and structures may all be a help, but they are not essential. God's way of life has been stamped on people's hearts; if they do not recognize it in their hearts, all the external expressions of religion will be useless to them.

Nowadays, reform is in the air. Through renewal, *aggiornamento*, or new forms of church structure, the Christian faith is being given a fresh look for modern man. There is everything to be said for it, for old trappings and out-of-date ways of expressing Christianity can obscure its eternal relevance. The externals can just as easily repel people as attract them, if they do not touch their actual way of life. But no external of religion, however relevant it may be, can replace religion itself. Religion is a matter of the heart.

This is not an easy lesson for any generation to learn, let alone the people with responsibility in religion – the pastors, priests, teachers and administrators of the various church structures. The man who first put this clearly was Jeremiah, and he spoke from bitter experience.

Early in Jeremiah's life, when he was still a young man, the king and the religious leaders brought in the most thorough reform of religion that the nation had ever known (there is a description of it in 2 Kings 22-23). All the truths of the old covenant were brought up to date; worship was carefully controlled from Jerusalem to keep it pure; religious duty was spelled out as the basis of social responsibility, and expressed in clear laws. All the authority of the state was used to make the reform work, and the young Jeremiah welcomed it with enthusiasm. It would bring the nation back to God again.

The reform failed, for within fourteen years the spirit had gone out of it. The people were left with magnificent outward forms, centred on the great Temple in Jerusalem, and a remarkable body of sacred law, but they were as far away from God as ever. If anything, the reform created a more dangerous condition: complacency. People felt that everything was all right, provided the services were maintained and the ceremonies of the religious laws observed. Religion easily became a matter of 'works', rather than a response to God from the heart.

Jeremiah's insight, as a result of this experience, was to look forward to a new covenant which would renew people's hearts: 'The days are coming (it is the Lord who speaks) when I will make a new covenant . . . Deep within them I will plant my Law, writing it on their hearts. Then I will be their God and they shall be my people.' (Jeremiah 31:32-3) By 'heart', Jeremiah and his fellow-Jews meant the innermost centre of the human personality where response begins, the deep ability to decide and to act, which is far more than mere emotions. God's way would be known to all, and would be known in a way which made it really effective. Spontaneous response to God's love would at last be possible, and it would be available to all.

Preaching is needed to tell people about God and the salvation he offers to his world, and preaching takes many forms. But there is no substitute for the personal response from the heart. Earlier in this letter (see 8:5-17) Paul has pointed out that we are not on our own in this response, this is not just another form of merely human effort. Through the Spirit, the human response is raised to the level of God's own love. But the response has to be there, as utter trust in the saving power of God. No external observance, or 'religious' act, can substitute for it.

Come to think of it, Paul had spelled this out two letters earlier, in the most famous passage he ever wrote (see 1 Corinthians 13). Even then, he was only echoing the teaching which Jesus gave again and again. All the effort the Pharisees put into their religion, and all they gave up for it, was a terrible waste of time unless it was motivated by love.

God's Mercy on Israel 11:1-12

Naturally enough, Jews are deeply irritated by what looks like Christian arrogance towards their religion. Christians are very ready to tell them that they have missed the point of their own religion. If they had really understood what God was saying to them, they would have welcomed Jesus the Christ when he came. However faithful the Jewish leaders may have been to their religion, they would never have had their Messiah crucified if they had grasped what their religion had to tell them. It is an easy line to take, and it is superficial.

We readily assume that great prophets such as Isaiah and Jeremiah were influential and successful in their own times. After all, we read them with approval, so the people who actually heard them must have been doubly impressed. Not so. Almost to a man, they seem to have made hardly any impression on their own generation. This is the point which Paul makes at this stage in his discussion of the Jewish problem. It is a point which has universal validity for Christians as well, as Paul will point out later (Romans 11:19-22).

Isaiah met with almost complete failure in the main crisis of his time. For the first time in their history, the Jews were facing a major international threat. The ruthless Assyrian military machine was beginning to roll down Palestine from the north, to control its frontiers with Egypt. The small Jewish kingdom of Judah was the last territory it would reach. It is a situation which all small powers have to face: what kind of alliance will guarantee survival? King Ahaz of Jerusalem chose to throw in his lot with the Assyrians before they reached his tiny country. Isaiah opposed him bitterly.

The Assyrian alliance would release a flood of paganism into the country, for it would be necessary to adopt the Assyrian religion to prove that the alliance was real. It would open the floodgates to every kind of degradation. Although the king was reigning from the throne of David, and was the main guardian of the covenant and the nation's religion, he turned his back on it all for the sake of national security. At some stage in his reign he even gave his own son as a burned sacrifice to the terrible god Moloch.

Nothing Isaiah could do would stop him, and the nation went into a hundred years (with only one brief respite) of appalling corruption. For Isaiah, this meant the end of the Hebrew monarchy as guardians of the

covenant. But it could not mean the end of God's love
for his people, or even the ultimate thwarting of God's
plans. So Isaiah began to look to the future, when God
would send a ruler and saviour who would bring his
people back to God again; it was the true beginning of
the teaching about a Messiah.

Meanwhile, the true faith would be preserved by a
small minority of the people, who would recognize the
terrible mistake being made by the national leaders.
They would be the 'remnant', through whom God would
still be working when everything seemed to be lost. (For
this whole episode, see Isaiah 7-12.)

Paul sees the Christians, still only a handful even at
the time when he is writing, as the remnant in his time.
Some of them are Jews, like Paul, who have accepted
Jesus as the Messiah; some are Gentiles, who show that
God is not limited by the methods he has used in the past.
The days of the Jews are over; their part in the plan has
ended. As individuals, some of them are now part of the
new minority, but it is no longer a national responsibility
for them. In God's good time, they will all return, but
meanwhile their history shows how God's blessings
become available even when everything seems to have
failed.

The Salvation of the Gentiles 11:13-24

Like every provident Hebrew family, Paul's parents saw
to it that their brilliant son was taught a trade. This part
of Paul's letter to the Roman Christians is sufficient to
show that his 'second-string' trade was not an agricultural one. In fact it was tent-making, and Paul's
handling of his agricultural example about grafting
starts from a mistaken idea of how it is done. The fruit
grower grafts his cultivated plant on to stronger wild
stock, not the other way round. But the point is well
made. The Gentiles are uncultivated, wild stock who are
now drawing on the strength of the carefully prepared
Hebrews.

There is no excuse for newcomers to God's plan if they
despise the Jews. The Jewish experience of nearly two
thousand years is essential for a proper understanding of
God's work in Jesus Christ. Before there was any New

Testament, Christians had scriptures to guide them in
their search for God. Their sacred books were the Old
Testament, which still forms by far the greater bulk of
the Christian Bible. They should be grateful for the experience which they have inherited.

They should be grateful, and they should be warned.
It is all too easy for Christians to fall into the same error
as the Jews, and complacently assume that they are
chosen by right. A man can no more be merely born into
the Christian relationship with God than a Jewish one. A
love relationship is never automatic; at every stage of its
development it depends on the love being returned.

There are many places in the gospels where this lesson
is spelled out by Jesus. It might be thought that his
disciples, and the inner group of the apostles, were the
ones who least needed to be reminded of it. But they too
were capable of thinking that they knew just how Jesus
should go about things, and that they had special rights.

Their ideas were shattered by the arrest of Jesus and the
crucifixion, but Jesus had needed to warn them well
before they arrived in Jerusalem for the last time. At
Caesarea Philippi, by the Sea of Galilee, he had warned
them that their journey down to Jerusalem would end
with humiliation and the most shameful death imagin-
able, before he achieved his victory.

They were appalled, and Peter tried to dissuade him,
only to receive the sternest of rebukes. Then Jesus turned
to the crowd, to tell everyone present what he had to offer
them: 'If anyone wants to come with me, he must forget
himself, carry his cross and follow me. For whoever
wants to save his own life will lose it; but whoever loses
his life for me and for the gospel will save it.' (Mark 8:
34-5)

In the end, the Jews had drifted away from God's
plan because they had become complacent about their
place in it. More seriously, it had not occurred to them
that they might be mistaken about the way in which God
intended to bring his salvation to the world. They were
content to guard their religion and ignore the world.
They became turned in on themselves, until the fence
they built round their faith prevented them from ful-
filling God's purpose.

When Jesus turned the traders out of the Temple, he

quoted from one of the greatest of the missionary passages in the Old Testament: 'Foreigners who have attached themselves to the Lord to serve him and to love his name and be his servants . . . these I will bring to my holy mountain. I will make them joyful in my house of prayer . . . for my house will be called a house of prayer for all the peoples.' (Isaiah 56:6-7) It was a promise which the Jews would not honour. Rather, they did all they could to exclude any foreigner, and any foreign influence, in case their way of life was threatened.

Christianity should be the most flexible of religions, for it offers God's way to all men. The Jewish origins of Christianity served their purpose, but the first Christians quickly realized that they must break away from them if they were truly to take God's salvation out into all the world. Yet the danger is always there that Christians in any age will turn their religion into a dead fossil, in which the structure and the form are preserved but the life has gone. Whenever that happens, they can expect to be treated in the way in which they think that God has treated the Jews. The next phase of the world's salvation will be achieved through strangers.

God's Mercy on All 11:25-32

From time to time, attempts are made to find a theory which will analyse the many threads of history and make plain the pattern which is being woven by them. The Marxist theory of historical determinism through dialectic is just such a theory which has had enormous influence on events in our own times. H. G. Wells' *The Outline of History* and, more recently, Arnold Toynbee's *A Study of History* have sought to make the patterns of history clear. In all ages there have been men who have seen God's hand in the events of their own times, to seek reassurance, or to confirm their beliefs that their own nations are of supreme importance.

All through this letter, Paul has been expounding a theory of history, but one which Christians believe has been revealed to the world by God himself. Jesus Christ is the key to history, for his approach to the world is God's approach, and from his life it is possible to understand the whole pattern of the creation. This is the secret which until the birth of Christ had been hidden, but is now plain for all to see if they will only look at the world from Christ's point of view.

It is a point of view which undermines human confidence in its own judgement, for by human standards of reasoning it is nonsense. The history of the world reaches its climax in a stable in Bethlehem, not in a Roman emperor's palace, and in a squalid execution rather than a spectacular military victory. The power at the heart of history is love, not force, and any one human being is as valuable as a whole empire. It does not assess the worth of people by their birth, their intelligence, their strength or their voting power. It gives them a value which has nothing to do with their achievements, whether they are potential or actual achievements. It is the value which God gives to each of them, out of the infinite mercy of his love, and it raises them to full fellowship with God himself.

On such a view, every aspect of history can be used by God to work towards the end he has planned. Disobedience, rebellion, rejection, only serve to show more clearly the quality of God's mercy as he continues to offer his love to the people who oppose him. Even those who accept him discover that they could only do so because God's love has evoked in them the response of love, and then amplified it until it matched the very love of God. The crucifixion and the triumph over death are the key to the world's progress, for the invincible God is the creator and sustainer of all things.

The last words Jesus addressed to his disciples in the Upper Room before his arrest, as John reports them, were words of triumph. He warned them that their loyalty would be tried beyond their endurance, and they would desert him. But they were not to worry. They would still share in Christ's victory, and his victory defeated anything which the world might pit against him. For Christ and the Father are one, and all things work together for good under their control.

Praise to God 11:33-6

The section of Paul's letter which examines the place of the Jews has come to its climax. He has surveyed the problem and put it into its proper perspective. There is not the slightest ground for any antisemitism in the view which Paul presents; quite the opposite. His nation has played a vital part in God's plan, and it is still close to his heart. It will only be a matter of time (and Paul thought it would be a very short time) before the whole plan reaches its final climax, and before that the Jews will have returned to their God. Meanwhile, they must be respected for what they have given to Christians.

Every aspect of the salvation of the world has been shown to be under the direct control of God, even when it seems to be working against him. If God acted by human logic, mankind would have been destroyed long ago. But the logic of love is the pattern which runs through history, so that all things point to God's glory. And in that logic, shown most clearly in Jesus Christ, man can be confident of salvation.

The only adequate action man can take in the face of such love is to worship. There is a mercy and a power here far beyond human understanding. All we know is that we have not deserved it, yet we are already sharing in the new life which God freely gives to us. The ultimate destiny and satisfaction for mankind is that it should use its new life to adore the one who gives it.

ROMANS 12:1-15:13

Life in God's Service

12 So then, my brothers, because of God's great mercy to us, I make this appeal to you: Offer yourselves as a living sacrifice to God, dedicated to his service and pleasing to him. This is the true worship that you should offer. [2]Do not conform outwardly to the standards of this world, but let God transform you inwardly by a complete change of your mind. Then you will be able to know the will of God—what is good, and is pleasing to him, and is perfect.

[3]And because of God's gracious gift to me, I say to all of you: Do not think of yourselves more highly than you should. Instead, be modest in your thinking, and each one of you judge himself according to the amount of faith that God has given him. [4]We have many parts in

the one body, and all these parts have different functions. ⁵In the same way, though we are many, we are one body in union with Christ and we are all joined to each other as different parts of one body. ⁶So we are to use our different gifts in accordance with the grace that God has given us. If our gift is to speak God's message, we must do it according to the faith that we have. ⁷If it is to serve, we must serve. If it is to teach, we must teach. ⁸If it is to encourage others, we must do so. Whoever shares with others what he has, must do it generously; whoever has authority, must work hard; whoever shows kindness to others, must do it cheerfully.

⁹Love must be completely sincere. Hate what is evil, hold on to what is good. ¹⁰Love one another warmly as brothers in Christ, and be eager to show respect for one another. ¹¹Work hard, and do not be lazy. Serve the Lord with a heart full of devotion. ¹²Let your hope keep you joyful, be patient in your troubles, and pray at all times. ¹³Share your belongings with your needy brothers, and open your homes to strangers.

¹⁴Ask God to bless those who persecute you; yes, ask him to bless, not to curse. ¹⁵Be happy with those who are happy, weep with those who weep. ¹⁶Have the same concern for all alike. Do not be proud, but accept humble duties. Do not think of yourselves as wise.

¹⁷If someone does evil to you, do not pay him back with evil. Try to do what all men consider to be good.

Never take revenge

[18]Do everything possible, on your part, to live at peace with all men. [19]Never take revenge, my friends, but instead let God's wrath do it. For the scripture says, "I will take revenge, I will pay back, says the Lord." [20]Instead, as the scripture says: "If your enemy is hungry, feed him; if he is thirsty, give him to drink; for by doing this you will heap burning coals on his head." [21]Do not let evil defeat you; instead, conquer evil with good.

Duties towards the State Authorities

13 Everyone must obey the state authorities, because no authority exists without God's permission, and the existing authorities have been put there by God. [2]Whoever opposes the existing authority opposes what God has ordered; and anyone who does so will bring judgment on himself. [3]For rulers are not to be feared by those who do good but by those who do evil. Would you like to be unafraid of the man in authority? Then do what is good, and he will praise you. [4]For he is God's servant working for your own good. But if you do evil, be afraid of him, because his power to punish is real. He is God's servant and carries out God's wrath on those who do evil. [5]For this reason you must obey the authorities—not just because of God's wrath, but also as a matter of conscience.

[6]This is also the reason that you pay taxes, because the authorities are working for God when they fulfil their duties. [7]Pay, then, what you owe them; pay them your personal and property taxes, and show respect and honour for them all.

Duties towards One Another

[8]Be in debt to no one—the only debt you should have is to love one another. Whoever loves his fellow-man has obeyed the Law. [9]The commandments, "Do not commit adultery; do not murder; do not steal; do not covet"—all these, and any others besides, are summed up in the one command, "Love your fellow-man as yourself." [10]Whoever loves his fellow-man will never do him wrong. To love, then, is to obey the whole Law.

[11]You must do this, because you know what hour it is: the time has come for you to wake up from your

sleep. For the moment when we will be saved is closer now than it was when we first believed. [12]The night is nearly over, day is almost here. Let us stop doing the things that belong to the dark, and take up the weapons for fighting in the light. [13]Let us conduct ourselves properly, as people who live in the light of day; no orgies or drunkenness, no immorality or indecency, no fighting or jealousy. [14]But take up the weapons of the Lord Jesus Christ, and stop giving attention to your sinful nature, to satisfy its desires.

Do Not Judge Your Brother

14 Accept among you the man who is weak in the faith, but do not argue with him about his personal opinions. [2]One man's faith allows him to eat anything, but the man who is weak in the faith eats only vegetables. [3]The man who will eat anything is not to despise the man who doesn't; while the one who eats only vegetables is not to pass judgment on the one who eats anything, because God has accepted him. [4]Who are you to judge the servant of someone else? It is his own Master who will decide whether he succeeds or fails. And he will succeed, because the Lord is able to make him succeed.

[5]One man thinks that a certain day is more important than the others, while another man thinks that all days are the same. Each one should have his own mind firmly made up. [6]Whoever thinks highly of a certain day does it in honour of the Lord; whoever eats anything does it in honour of the Lord, because he gives thanks to God for the food. Whoever refuses to eat certain things does so in honour of the Lord, and he gives thanks to God. [7]None of us lives for himself only, none of us dies for himself only; [8]if we live, it is for the Lord that we live, and if we die, it is for the Lord that we die. Whether we live or die, then, we belong to the Lord. [9]For Christ died and rose to life in order to be the Lord of the living and of the dead. [10]You, then—why do you pass judgment on your brother? And you—why do you despise your brother? All of us will stand before God, to be judged by him. [11]For the scripture says,

"As I live, says the Lord,
everyone will kneel before me,

and everyone will confess that I am
　　　God."
[12]Every one of us, then, will have to give an account of
himself to God.

Do Not Make Your Brother Fall

[13]So then, let us stop judging one another. Instead,
this is what you should decide: not to do anything that
would make your brother stumble, or fall into sin. [14]My
union with the Lord Jesus makes me know for certain
that nothing is unclean of itself; but if a man believes
that something is unclean, then it becomes unclean for
him. [15]If you hurt your brother because of something
you eat, then you are no longer acting from love. Do not
let the food that you eat ruin the man for whom Christ
died! [16]Do not let what you regard as good acquire a bad
name. [17]For God's Kingdom is not a matter of eating
and drinking, but of the righteousness, peace, and joy
that the Holy Spirit gives. [18]And whoever serves Christ
in this way wins God's pleasure and man's approval.

[19]So then, we must always aim at those things that
bring peace, and that help strengthen one another.
[20]Do not, because of food, destroy what God has done.
All foods may be eaten, but it is wrong to eat anything
that will cause someone else to fall into sin. [21]The right
thing to do is to keep from eating meat, drinking wine,
or doing anything else
that will make your
brother fall. [22]Keep what
you believe about this
matter, then, between
yourself and God. Happy
is the man who does not
feel himself condemned
when he does what he ap-
proves of! [23]But if he has
doubts about what he
eats, God condemns him
when he eats it, because
his action is not based on
faith. And anything that
is not based on faith is
sin.

Help the weak

Please Others, Not Yourselves

15 We who are strong in the faith ought to help the weak to carry their burdens. We should not please ourselves. [2]Instead, each of us should please his brother for his own good, in order to build him up in the faith. [3]For Christ did not please himself. Instead, as the scripture says, "The insults spoken by those who insulted you have fallen on me." [4]Everything written in the Scriptures was written to teach us, in order that we might have hope through the patience and encouragement the Scriptures give us. [5]And may God, the source of patience and encouragement, enable you to have the same point of view among yourselves by following the example of Christ Jesus, [6]so that all of you together, with one voice, may praise the God and Father of our Lord Jesus Christ.

The Gospel to the Gentiles

[7]Accept one another, then, for the glory of God, as Christ has accepted you. [8]Because I tell you that Christ became a servant of the Jews to show that God is faithful, to make God's promises to the patriarchs come true, [9]and also to enable the Gentiles to praise God for his mercy. As the scripture says,

"And so I will give thanks to you among
        the Gentiles,
    I will sing praises to your name."
[10]Again it says,
    "Rejoice, Gentiles, with God's chosen
        people!"
[11]And again,
    "Praise the Lord, all Gentiles;
        praise him, all peoples!"
[12]And again, Isaiah says,
    "A descendant of Jesse will come;
        he will be raised to rule the Gentiles,
        and they will put their hope in him."
[13]May God, the source of hope, fill you with all joy and peace by means of your faith in him, so that your hope will continue to grow by the power of the Holy Spirit.

Section 6: Practical Advice for Life in Christ

Romans 12:1-15:13

When Paul settled down to write his letter to the Christians in Rome, his main purpose was to set down the Christian gospel as he taught it in his missionary work. He wanted to make Rome his home base, from which he could spread the Good News of Jesus Christ throughout the western part of the Roman Empire. Many of the Christians in Rome had already met him on their travels, and many more would certainly have heard about him, but it was important that they should know just what Paul thought.

Paul needed to be sure that the Roman Christians understood his position, particularly about the place of non-Jews in God's plan of salvation. The Roman Jews had no time for Christians, understandably, and when Paul finally reached Rome and made contact with the Jews there they told him that 'all we know about this sect is that opinion everywhere condemns it.' (Acts 28:22) Paul would have to explain himself both to the Jews and to the Christians, if he wanted their confidence.

The greater part of Paul's letter is concerned with the basic principles of the gospel, as we have seen. Now he can turn to the practical consequences of it in everyday life. From the beginning, Christianity has always been a strongly social gospel, with important consequences for the way in which people treat each other – whether the others are Christians or not. Whenever this side of the gospel has been ignored it has been a sure sign that the basic principles were being ignored as well. There is nothing to stop people calling themselves Christians, but it does not always follow that they have accepted the consequences of Christ's teaching, or even the beliefs from which the consequences flow.

Having established the basic teaching of the gospel, Paul can now turn to the consequences which flow from it. What kind of lives do Christians lead? It is a remarkably tolerant picture which Paul presents, with room for a very wide range of practices. People come in all shapes and sizes; they have just as many ways of expressing themselves and their love for God. Paul gives no support to rigid uniformity in public worship or in private devotions. In fact, he suggests that the only real restriction should be one we impose on ourselves out of consideration for others. We should do nothing which is likely to weaken the faith of others who do not see things in quite the same way.

Running through all that Paul has to say is a deep feeling for the community. Christians are not living out their love for God in isolation from each other. They are linked together by bonds which God has made, in a brotherhood far stronger than any merely human one, and this is the basis of their relationships with each other. They are the body of Christ, so that the life of Christ in all its strength and fulness will be shown in their lives.

It is commonly believed that a prophet is someone who can see into the future and tell people how God's plans for them will work out. It is much more important to see prophets as men and women who can apply God's truths to their present situation, and spell out the consequences of God's love for their own times. In this sense, Paul is a prophet. He applies the new covenant, the gospel, to his own life, and to the lives of the Christians for whom he had been given responsibility. Amos, Hosea, Isaiah, Jeremiah and all the great Hebrew prophets of the old covenant had done just that for their own times. In the same way, Paul shows how the practical details of Christian living derive from the life and teaching of Jesus.

Paul was a Roman citizen and by this time, a man of deep practical experience of the world and its ways. He could earn his living, and did, at a manual trade. In the twenty years that he had been a Christian, Paul had come to grips with the practical needs of Christians in dozens of different places and had accepted pastoral responsibility for them. Situations change, and we are not living in the Roman Empire of nearly two thousand years ago, so there may be times when we feel that the advice given by Paul does not fit our own particular needs. But the Christian gospel does not change, and all Christians have a duty to apply it in their everyday lives. Paul has a great deal to teach us about the way to apply the teaching of Christ to our own situation, whatever it may be.

Life in God's Service 12:1-21

There has always been a danger, in religion, that 'worship' may be given a very narrow meaning. 'Divine Worship' on a church notice-board can convey this impression all too easily. It is seen as a series of outward acts, or the giving of a regular and limited amount of time, which fulfils the obligations to God. The rest of the time is then your own, to do what you want.

That is certainly an extreme view, held by no one with any sense of God in their lives. But the tendency for religion to deteriorate into this is there, all the same. Most of the prophets of the Old Testament found that they had to condemn this in their own times, as they watched their people go faithfully to the sacrifices and then cheat and bribe their way through the rest of their lives.

The real connection between religion and life shows, in this part of Paul's letter, when it is realized that there can be no compromise between sacrifice and the standards of this world. The sacrifice of Jesus is not to be seen solely in his death at Calvary. It shows in every word and every act of his throughout his life, as he applies his understanding of God to the events of everyday living. It is a quality of life rather than a manner of death.

This quality of life requires a transformation of human nature, which people cannot achieve by themselves. They must make the effort, and must truly want to act by God's standards, but the transformation which actually makes it possible for them is yet another act of God's love.

Throughout this part of the letter, Paul will be drawing on the experiences and the teaching which he expressed in earlier letters. Already, in 1 Corinthians 12, he had written extensively about the way in which people are united together by the share which each of them has in the life of Jesus. Their union with Christ makes them into parts of one body, so that God can communicate with his world through them. As they grow into their union with Christ, so they become more like him in their thinking and their actions, and this is the way in which their nature is transformed. There is nothing forced about it, nothing which is done against their will or without their co-operation. In fact, they will find themselves able to act with more and more freedom and sincerity as they grow closer to the mind of God.

Thus it is no accident that these parts of this letter are so reminiscent of the Sermon on the Mount (Matthew 5-7). In that part of the gospel, there is a summary of the kind of teaching which Jesus used to give to the crowds who flocked out to hear him. They were presented with ideal standards in which there is no compromise with imperfect or weak human nature. In the end, there is no need for compromise, for the Good News that Jesus declared contains the essential factor which makes the ideal standard practicable. Those who share in the life of Jesus are eventually able to love as he loved, and they experience something of this transformation from the beginning.

Duties towards the State Authorities 13:1-7

When Paul was writing this letter, Rome was still tolerant towards Christians; in fact, it is doubtful whether the Roman authorities thought of Christians as anything more than a kind of Jewish sect. And the Romans were extraordinarily tolerant towards Jews, perhaps because they first went to Syria and Palestine to fulfil the obligations of a treaty between Rome and the Jewish State.

Christians had run into trouble from the beginning, but it came from the Jewish authorities, or from local communities which felt that the new teaching might be threatening their way of life. The first real clash with the central Roman government did not come until AD 64, when Nero blamed the Christians for the great fire which destroyed so much of Rome. Popular rumour had it that Christians indulged in cannibalism, so there was no need for surprise that other crimes might be committed by them.

From Nero onwards, outbreaks of official persecution were common, especially as emperor-worship grew, for Christians could not accept any other god without denying the fundamental teachings of the gospel. Not until the conversion of the Emperor Constantine, more than three hundred years after the birth of Christ, was it safe to be known as a Christian in the Roman Empire.

Perhaps Paul would have been a little less sure that 'rulers are not to be feared by those who do good but by

those who do evil' if he had lived in less tolerant times.
Even so, some form of stable social structure is essential
for human beings, and Christianity has never laid down
any principles which make one form of government
better than another. In Paul's time, the essential equality
of Christians was to be found through their union with
Christ (as in Galatians 3:28) rather than in political
equality.

There is a lesson here about the limitations of Christian
thinking in any one period of history, and about the use
of Christianity for political ends. For Paul and his fellow-
Christians, there was no essential contradiction between
Christianity and slavery, provided that Christians did
not regard slaves as inferior beings; clearly, this line of
thought would not be acceptable to Christians today.

From the earliest times, people have tried to use the
gospel for purely political ends, whether to suppress their
fellow-men or to support violent civic disobedience. In
either case, the point of the gospel is missed. By a careful
selection of texts, almost any course of political action
can be 'proved' from the New Testament. The truth is at
a deeper level. There can be no compromise with the
truth of God, and with the value which the gospel places
on each individual human being. But Jesus defended this
truth by going to his death for it, and showing that the
love by which he lived was stronger than any political
force and more important than any political structure.
Paul died, so tradition says, by the hand of the Roman
State for being a Christian, but he would not have had
the Roman State overthrown for that.

Duties towards One Another 13:8-14

Echoes from the gospels become stronger than ever, perhaps because so much of the teaching that Jesus gave had
already been expressed in the highest forms of Judaism.
The Christian teaching about relationships between
people would already have been familiar to Paul from his
studies in Jewish law.

Thus when the lawyer challenged Jesus to give him a
formula for eternal life, Jesus could turn the question
back to the questioner: 'What do the scriptures say [i.e.,
the Old Testament]? How do you interpret them?' In
answer, the lawyer quoted from Deuteronomy 6:5 and

Leviticus 19:18: ' "You must love the Lord your God
with all your heart, with all your soul, with all your
strength, and with all your mind"; and, "You must love
your fellow-man as yourself." ' (Luke 10:27) It was an
answer which could have been given by any devout Jew,
and by many adherents of other of the ancient religions
of the world.

Christianity gives this teaching a new edge by linking
it with the sheer power of Christ. For the sinful nature of
man, unaided, such a summary of eternal life must be a
pipe-dream; but by the help of Christ it becomes as
practicable a programme for human beings as it was for
Jesus himself.

A new urgency was given to the old teaching by the
beliefs of the first Christians that time was running out at
an alarming speed. At any moment, Christ would return
to bring his work to its completion. His power was
already there, transforming the world, but the opportunity to benefit from it was shortening every moment:
'The night is nearly over, day is almost here.' (13:12)
Love gives opportunity for response, and for growth into
the perfection which love offers, but it is not an unlimited
opportunity.

We no longer think in this literal and urgent way about
the return of Christ, yet the world's need for Christ's
power of love was never more urgent than it is today.
The belief that there is only a limited opportunity to
bring people to God, and to grow into his love, is a
powerful spur. There are many places in the gospels,
such as the parables of watchfulness (Luke 12:35-48),
where Jesus conveys just such a sense of urgency.

Do Not Judge Your Brother 14:1-12

In 1 Corinthians, Paul answers a question put to him
about eating meat which had been sacrificed to a pagan
god. Was it contaminated? For Paul this opened up the
whole question of freedom within religion, and he
answered the Corinthians' question in a way which under-
lined both Christian freedom and Christian responsibility.

It is always a temptation to try to reduce human
behaviour to clear rules and authoritative laws, if only to
give people a chance of judging how successful they are.
Every major form of Christianity has fallen into this trap

at some point or other, and for many it is still the hall-
mark of religion. Commandments, usually in the form of
prohibitions, seem to be an inevitable consequence of
discovering God in this world.

In this part of his letter, Paul defends a very wide
range of religious observance. It is so wide, in fact, that
no one can judge the faith of anyone else. If they are
honestly behaving as they do in order to honour God,
that is all that matters; their motives and achievements
will be judged by God, and mere men should not be
concerned about them.

People have to be judged by what God thinks of them;
the Christian approach towards other people can never
be wrong if it leans towards compassion and tolerance
of other beliefs conscientiously held. It must have been
an enormous relief for Paul when he finally found release
from a religion which spelled out religious duties in great
detail, and judged its members by their success in keeping
the religious laws. In his meeting with Christ on the
Damascus Road, Paul glimpsed a deeper and more
personal way of approaching God, through his Son
Jesus Christ. Christ enlightens all men, and offers them
as many ways of approaching God as their differing
circumstances and needs make appropriate.

There is only one fundamental limitation of this universal freedom in religion, and to this Paul turns next.

Do Not Make Your Brother Fall 14:13-23

In his discussion of the Corinthians' problem about food
'polluted' by association with pagan sacrifices, Paul told
them not to worry. They knew, as faithful Christians,
that God is the creator and sustainer of the whole
universe, so there was no other real power to cause the
pollution. They should eat and stop worrying, if it only
affected themselves (1 Corinthians 8-10).

The real responsibilities of the Christian way of life
emerge more fully when we stop to consider the effects of
our actions on people who are less certain about things.
If there is any danger of undermining the faith of anyone
else, then, says Paul, love compels us to act with caution.
We are not solitary individuals; we are in a brotherhood
which creates responsibilities for each other, and these

responsibilities should govern our decisions about what we do.

The test of action is to be peace. At first sight, this seems like an intolerable limitation of freedom, but in practice it disarms opposition and strengthens those who feel that their faith is being undermined. There is a grave responsibility not to lead others into sin.

Paul takes this responsibility much farther than many of us would be prepared to take it. He says that Christians should even be sensitive to what others consider sinful, even if they do not feel that way about it themselves. If they ignore this kind of obligation, they may lead others to do things which they think are sinful, and thus injure people who are not so clear in conscience. This would be a breach of love.

The only sure guide to action is the attitude towards God which is summed up by the word 'faith'. This attitude comes from a realization of human helplessness and the need for God's saving love. If a person has any real doubts about the rightness of his or her actions, it is very probable that the course of action is wrong. Without God, we inevitably act wrongly, and the only sensible course is to recognize this fact. Once we face ourselves, we discover the love which God offers to us as the source of right decision and of the ability to carry it out.

Please Others, Not Yourselves 15:1-6

The point Paul has been making is continued here, but in an even more positive way. Christians have a duty to avoid actions which undermine others, but they have a positive responsibility to encourage others and help them to cope with the Christian life.

Read in the right way, this can be seen as one of the main experiences to which the Old Testament points. The most common and logical of human attitudes is the hope for justice, in which goodness will be rewarded and wrong-doing punished. By an extension, it is natural to assume that a just God will make sure that those who obey him are prosperous, and that misfortune will fall on those who ignore or oppose him.

Several important books of the Old Testament question this logic on the grounds that it contradicts common experience. Job insists that he is innocent, despite his

friends' insistence that he must have deserved the suffering which has fallen upon him. The author of Ecclesi-
astes goes even further than Job in holding that God's
ways are beyond human understanding.

Only one author, and a few places in the Psalms, suggest that there is a deeper logic to misfortune. The
author is the anonymous poet whose work is contained
in Isaiah 40-55, where in four 'Songs of the Servant'
(Isaiah 42:1-4; 49:1-6; 50:4-9; 52:13-53:12) he suggests
that it is the innocent who suffer precisely because they
are faithful to God, and that they help others to bear their
misfortunes. At one point, he even says that the innocent
can bear suffering on behalf of those who deserve it, and
by so doing the innocent bring about the salvation of the
wrong-doers.

It seems very likely that the poet was thinking of the
whole Jewish nation when he wrote. To some extent their
sufferings were undeserved, yet they helped to bring other
peoples to God. At least, it could be that their witness to
God's way of life in a hostile world aroused opposition,
but this only served to show the strength of the love by
which they lived.

This is certainly a point which Paul had made about
suffering, throughout 2 Corinthians, and earlier in this
letter to the Romans (Romans 5:3-5). An athlete does
not know the full extent of the strength at his disposal
until he has experienced the strongest of challenges. So
too, suffering brings out the full extent of the love which
God shares with man.

This love is shared, not only by God with man, but by
people with each other, as they help each other and
suffer for each other. It is one of the aspects of the
Christian life which point to a sharing in the life and experiences of Jesus, both on earth and in his heavenly
glory. And it is the experience which assures the Christian
that he or she is part of a larger community, united in the
worship of God. In this respect, all divisions are tran-
scended and we are one in Jesus Christ.

The Gospel to the Gentiles 15:7-13

Paul has now reached another natural pause in his
thoughts, as he rounds off his advice about the practical
implications of the Good News for those who accept it.

There was one such pause at the end of chapter 8, and another at the end of chapter 11, when Tertius could pack up for the day in his work of writing this letter at Paul's dictation.

As before, Paul is overwhelmed by the scope of God's plan for his world, and by the patience with which God pursues man's salvation. The toleration which Christians show to their fellow-men is no more than a pale shadow of the patience and flexibility of God.

Once again, Jesus is the key which opens the innermost secrets of God's plans. The long years of preparation, from Abraham right down to Joseph and Mary, were only the beginnings. Now it is possible to look back and see something of the whole development.

Jesus was born a Jew, but this was only to bring that part of the plan to its completion. The pattern of life which God showed to the founders of the Hebrew nation was brought to its perfection in Jesus. Then it was thrown open to the world. All the elements of exclusiveness were removed, and the Good News of salvation has begun to echo round the world. The invitation is universal; the only qualification needed is to acknowledge the need for God's saving love, and to put one's entire trust in God alone.

The result is far beyond anything that imagination could invent: the joy and peace which come from the experience of God's saving love, and the growing realization that the deepest of human hopes will be fulfilled. Earlier in this letter, Paul has written that 'God's Spirit joins himself to our spirits to declare that we are God's children.' (Romans 8:16) Jesus himself showed what that meant by the whole of his life and by his victory over death itself. To share in love of that magnitude, and to the full, is the central truth of the Good News.

ROMANS 15:14-16:27

Paul's Reason for Writing So Boldly

[14]My brothers: I myself feel sure that you are full of goodness, that you are filled with all knowledge and are able to teach one another. [15]But in this letter I have been quite bold about certain subjects of which I have re-

minded you. I have been bold because of the privilege God has given me [16]of being a servant of Christ Jesus to work for the Gentiles. I serve like a priest in preaching the Good News from God, in order that the Gentiles may be an offering acceptable to God, dedicated to him by the Holy Spirit. [17]In union with Christ Jesus, then, I can be proud of my service for God. [18]I will be bold and speak only of what Christ has done through me to lead the Gentiles to obey God, by means of words and deeds, [19]by the power of signs and miracles, and by the power of the Spirit. And so, in travelling all the way from Jerusalem to Illyricum, I have proclaimed fully the Good News about Christ. [20]My ambition has always been to proclaim the Good News in places where Christ has not been heard of, so as not to build on the foundation laid by someone else. [21]As the scripture says,

"Those who were not told about him will
       see,
             and those who have not heard will understand."

Paul's Plan to Visit Rome

[22]For this reason I have been prevented many times from coming to you. [23]But now that I have finished my work in these regions, and since I have been wanting for so many years to come to see you, [24]I hope to do so now. I would like to see you on my way to Spain, and be helped by you to go there, after I have enjoyed visiting you for a while. [25]Right now, however, I am going to Jerusalem in the service of God's people there. [26]For the churches in Macedonia and Greece have freely decided to give an offering to help the poor among God's people in Jerusalem. [27]They themselves decided to do it. But, as a matter of fact, they have an obligation to help those poor; the Jews shared their spiritual blessings with the Gentiles, and so the Gentiles ought to serve the Jews with their material blessings. [28]When I have finished this task, and have turned over to them the full amount of money that has been raised for them, I shall leave for Spain and visit you on my way there. [29]When I come to you, I know that I shall come with a full measure of the blessing of Christ.

[30]I urge you, brothers, by our Lord Jesus Christ and

by the love that the Spirit gives: join me in praying fervently to God for me. [31]Pray that I may be kept safe from the unbelievers in Judea, and that my service in Jerusalem may be acceptable to God's people there. [32]And so I will come to you full of joy, if it is God's will, and enjoy a refreshing visit with you. [33]May God, our source of peace, be with all of you. Amen.

Personal Greetings

16 I recommend to you our sister Phoebe, who serves the church at Cenchreae. [2]Receive her in the Lord's name, as God's people should, and give her any help she may need from you; for she herself has been a good friend to many people and also to me.

[3]I send greetings to Priscilla and Aquila, my fellow workers in the service of Christ Jesus, [4]who risked their lives for me. I am grateful to them—not only I, but all the Gentile churches as well. [5]Greetings also to the church that meets in their house.

Greetings to my dear friend Epaenetus, who was the first man in the province of Asia to believe in Christ. [6]Greetings to Mary, who has worked so hard for you. [7]Greetings to Andronicus and Junias, fellow Jews who were in prison with me; they are well known among the apostles, and they became Christians before I did.

[8]My greetings to Ampliatus, my dear friend in the fellowship of the Lord. [9]Greetings to Urbanus, our fellow worker in Christ's service, and to Stachys, my dear friend. [10]Greetings to Apelles, whose loyalty to Christ has been proved. Greetings to those who belong to the family of Aristobulus. [11]Greetings to Herodion, a fellow Jew, and to the Christian brothers in the family of Narcissus.

[12]My greetings to Tryphaena and Tryphosa, who work in the Lord's service, and to my dear friend Persis, who has done so much work for the Lord. [13]I send greetings to Rufus, that outstanding worker in the Lord's service, and to his mother, who has always treated me like a son. [14]My greetings to Asyncritus, Phlegon, Hermes, Patrobas, Hermas, and all the other Christian brothers with them. [15]Greetings to Philologus and Julia, to Nereus and his sister, to Olympas and to all of God's people who are with them.

[16]Greet one another with a brotherly kiss. All the churches of Christ send you their greetings.

Final Instructions

[17]I urge you, my brothers: watch out for those who cause divisions and upset people's faith, who go against the teaching which you have received; keep away from them. [18]For those who do such things are not serving Christ our Lord, but their own appetites. By their fine words and flattering speech they deceive the minds of innocent people. [19]Everyone has heard of your loyalty to the gospel, and for this reason I am happy about you. I want you to be wise about what is good, but innocent in what is evil. [20]And God, our source of peace, will soon crush Satan under your feet.

The grace of our Lord Jesus be with you.

[21]Timothy, my fellow worker, sends you his greetings; and so do Lucius, Jason, and Sosipater, fellow Jews.

[22]I, Tertius, the writer of this letter, send you Christian greetings.

[23]My host Gaius, in whose house the church meets, sends you his greetings; Erastus, the city treasurer, and our brother Quartus, send you their greetings.

[[24]The grace of our Lord Jesus Christ be with you all. Amen.]

Concluding Prayer of Praise

[25]Let us give glory to God! He is able to make you stand firm in your faith, according to the Good News I preach, the message about Jesus Christ, and according to the revelation of the secret truth which was hidden for long ages in the past. [26]Now, however, that truth has been brought out into the open through the writings of the prophets; and by the command of the eternal God it is made known to all nations, so that all may believe and obey.

[27]To the only God, who alone is all-wise, be the glory through Jesus Christ forever! Amen.

Section 7: Plans, Greetings and Conclusion

Romans 15:14-16:27

The final parts of Paul's letter to the Christians of Rome are full of personal information about his plans and hopes. For three-quarters of this letter, Paul has set out the Christian faith as he preached it. From the calm of Corinth, with the tensions between himself and the Corinthian Christians resolved, Paul could look back over the twenty turbulent years that he had been a Christian.

For most of that time he had been on the move, taking the Good News of Jesus Christ into places which had not yet heard it, and laying the foundations for local Christian communities. In the course of it all, he had made many discoveries about the risen life of Christ and its implications for life in this world. Not least, he had learned much about suffering and its relationship to the love of God. Paul's summary of the Christian gospel was based on the experience of living it.

The main purpose in writing this letter has been achieved. He has established that Christians from very different backgrounds are all speaking about the same basic truths and are believing in the same saving events. But even in these closing chapters, the basic Christian truths are to be seen just below the surface. We see Paul using them naturally, to illuminate his practical decisions and to explain his whole approach to his work. The casual way in which he refers to profound truths shows how closely they are woven into the very fabric of his being.

He is an apostle, entrusted with the work of God and living out the apostolic life of Jesus as he goes about his work. He is a priest, whose special offering to God is the whole of the Gentile world. He is a member of the universal Christian community, and that community's life in every aspect is so saturated with the life of Christ that there is no longer any gulf between the material life and the spiritual. Paul can plan to travel to the farthest reaches of the Roman Empire, and beyond, confident that the Christian way of salvation will make sense to all people, no matter how or where they live.

In the gospels, the majesty and glory of Jesus can be seen in everything he does and says, not merely in the moments when he is caught up in such supernatural events as the transfiguration (Matthew 17:1-13). Once his followers know what to look for (and this calls for a thorough change in their ideas about God), they begin to realize that this is God amongst them, expressing himself in a thoroughly human way.

The same glory, expressed in ordinary human lives, is to be seen in the people who believe in Jesus. At one time, says Paul, people thought that God's glory was hidden. Jesus has changed all that. Not only has he revealed it, he has also shared it. The love of God is there in the world for all to recognize, once they know where to look for it; its overwhelming power and security have been demonstrated by Jesus, the Son of God; to share in this is to share in the glory of God and to taste the ultimate perfection of love, for which God made man.

Paul's Reasons for Writing So Boldly 15:14-21

Paul has written to the Christians of Rome with confidence. After the long analysis of his apostolic authority, which Paul made in the last letter he wrote (2 Corinthians), it comes as no surprise that he does not think this authority comes from any special abilities of his own. He writes with confidence because God has made him his servant.

The results of God's trust are to be seen in the work Paul has already done throughout the eastern end of the Roman Empire. He can feel with justification that he has been more than a mere servant. He feels that in this work he is a priest who has consecrated a special offering and brought it to God. The offering is the Gentile world, the great mass of people who were outside 'the Law'. They have been consecrated to God through the Good News which Paul has preached to them. He has been the means whereby they have been brought within the power of God's holiness. He feels, rightly, that Christ has drawn him into his own work of saving the world.

At the most sacred moment in ancient Hebrew history, immediately after the escape from Egypt under the leadership of Moses, very similar language is used. The Hebrews were told by God, 'I will count you a kingdom of priests, a consecrated nation.' (Exodus 19:6) They were called to recognize God's love, to respond to it themselves, and to share it with the rest of the world.

Now that nation has been expanded, and it is clear that the old divisions have been broken down. In words which echo those of Moses and of Paul, Peter writes in the same way to the new nation of Christians consecrated to God: 'You are the chosen race, the King's priests, the holy nation, God's own people, chosen to proclaim the wonderful acts of God, who called you from the darkness into his own marvellous light.' (1 Peter 2:9)

Salvation is not a release from responsibilities but an entry into them. The priesthood of Christ, in which he consecrated himself to his Father's service, is shared with all Christians, so that all can share in his work of bringing the world back to God again. Paul is doing priestly work, as he spreads the Good News of Jesus, and takes care that it is always in new places so that God's love may spread as swiftly as possible. The result is to open up new opportunities for consecrated service in the people whom he has brought to God.

There is a sense of urgency about it all. Time is running out. There is a whole world to be consecrated to God. No one could pretend that this same sense of urgency is felt amongst Christians today, yet each new generation is a world to be consecrated to God. Could it be that many people, particularly in the western world, feel that they have been born into Christianity and automatically inherit its benefits? If so, they are falling into the same error which Jesus condemned in the Jews of his own time, and for which he was crucified.

Paul's Plan to Visit Rome 15:22-33

Quite casually, in this part of his letter, Paul takes for granted a most important principle of Christian fellowship. In fact, he takes for granted that fellowship itself.

There are many different things which can draw people together. They may be related by blood, live in the same district or country, or be interested in doing the same things. Such factors can be the reason for a family, a nation or a club. We all of us belong to a number of different kinds of human association, each of them based on something we have in common with the other members.

The Christian community is unique amongst human associations, for it is based on the share which each of its members has in the life of Christ. The closest human comparison is the family, where the members are held together by the share which each of them has in the life of the parents. We do not select our brothers and sisters; nor do we select our fellow-Christians. Our relationships with them are created by the relationship which each of them (and us) has with God.

Just as the members of a family accept obligations for each other, so too with the Christian fellowship. Paul shows this in a remarkable way at this point in his letter. The Greek word for fellowship is *koinonia*, and Paul uses this same word for the collection or offering that the Christians of Greece have made to help the Christians of Jerusalem. The money they have raised is more than a mere material aid to Christians in distress. It is a symbol of the fellowship of Christ to which they all belong. The Jewish Christians have given the Gentiles all the riches of the Good News of their salvation in Christ; the material gifts from the Gentiles are an apt expression of their common life in the body of Christ.

Paul tells the Christians of Rome that he wants to come to them as soon as possible, to start his missionary work in the other half of the Roman Empire, but first he must return to Jerusalem to deliver the money he has collected.

Does Paul have a premonition of disaster as he writes these words? Perhaps; for he was arrested in Jerusalem soon after his arrival there, and only reached Rome as a prisoner waiting for the Emperor to hear his appeal.

There are many places in Paul's letters where he writes movingly about the fellowship which binds Christians together. It is a fellowship which is far more fundamental, and far wider, than the divisions which separate the various Christian organizations, for it is created by Christ himself. So it is not surprising that the fullest expression of this fellowship in the New Testament is to be found in Christ's own words, in the teaching Jesus gave in the Upper Room immediately before his arrest (John 15), and in the prayer with which he consecrated himself to the Father who had sent him into the world (John 17).

The characteristic mark of this fellowship, as Jesus taught, is love. It was the fundamental power which Paul discovered in it. It is still the only fundamental test for recognizing God's presence in Christian organizations which sometimes seem to be all too worldly and human.

Personal Greetings 16:1-16

The list of people to whom Paul sends his greetings gives us some idea of the way in which the Christian faith spread, and may even tell us how the church in Rome developed.

Christians met in each others' houses at this time, and the very shape of the first churches, when they were finally built, was modelled on a typical Roman house. In Rome, the Christians met in the house of Priscilla and Aquila, who are also mentioned several times in the Acts of the Apostles (see chapter 18). They were Jews whom Paul first met in Corinth, where they were staying after the Emperor Claudius had expelled the Jews from Rome. Like Paul, Aquila was a tent-maker, and they gave Paul hospitality. No doubt they had heard him when he preached in the Jewish synagogue in Corinth, and they became Christians.

Later (Acts 18:24-6), they in their turn were able to take an important part in the spread of the gospel. For a short while, they accompanied Paul after he left Corinth, and then settled for a while in Ephesus; now, it seems, they have been able to return to Rome, and have become leading members of the Christian community there. It is an interesting insight into the mobility which helped Christianity to grow.

The mention of Phoebe shows how quickly women were able to play an important part in church life. It was not long before they were given official positions with a recognized ministry. The Greek word *diakonos* is used to describe her work; in this translation it is expressed by the general word 'serves', rather than 'deaconess', but this special ministry may already have developed.

There is a mixture of Jews and Gentiles, showing that the old divisions which, for a while, persisted in the Christian community itself, have gone. Since these people are all friends of Paul, it is not surprising that some of them were converted by him in other parts of the Empire, and some have even shared his many imprisonments (see 2 Corinthians 11:23).

The 'brotherly kiss' which Paul mentions may show that this letter would be read at the Eucharist, when the Christians gathered to celebrate the Lord's Supper. Near the moment when they received communion, those present showed their unity and their love for each other with a kiss.

Final Instructions 16:17-24

Paul is writing this letter from Corinth, so it is not surprising that his experiences with the Christians of Corinth are at the front of his mind. They were very dear to him, but they had almost wrecked his work amongst them by their quarrels and divisions. The first of the two letters of Paul to Corinth opens with three chapters of rebuke and worry about the factions and parties in the Corinthian church, and at one stage they came near rejecting Paul himself.

So Paul warns the Christians of Rome against the kind of people who cause splits in the Christian community. There is an enormously broad spirit of tolerance about Paul. He knows that there are many different kinds of temperament and taste amongst human beings, and no one way of doing things will appeal to all. In worship and in the language of the faith, there are many different ways of expressing the truth. It is a sad irony that Paul, the man who saw this danger so clearly, has been used so often as a support for divisions.

The history of Christianity has many terrible examples of quarrels and differences which have split Christians, and of terrible persecutions of Christians by each other. Thank God, there are signs in our own times that some of the narrow-minded faction thinking of the past is being rejected, and Christians who think differently and worship differently are able to see the good in each other and agree on fundamentals.

Just for a moment, we catch a glimpse of the scribe who wrote this letter at Paul's dictation. He too, it seems, had many friends amongst the Christians of Rome. If he was Paul's regular secretary, who travelled with him and looked after his copious correspondence, he would have met many of the Roman Christians on his travels. So Tertius, 'the writer of this letter', sends his greetings.

Concluding Prayer of Praise 16:25-7

The last words of Paul in this letter are centred on glory, and they turn the mind back to God.

Promises are only as good as the person who makes them. In our modern world of credit cards, monthly accounts and mortgages, we have become all too familiar with the idea of 'credit worthiness'. A garage, a store, a building society check around before they trust us. They write to our employers, the bank we use and other traders with whom we deal to see whether we normally honour our commitments. In a word, they want to know whether our promises carry weight.

'Weight' is the root meaning which lies far back in the origins of the idea of 'glory'. It expresses the power, the importance and the authority of a king. It sums up the wealth and influence of a citizen. Joseph, in the Genesis story of how the Hebrews went to Egypt, was able to show his brethren 'all the glory' he had acquired in Egypt (Genesis 45:13); they could safely bring their father to Egypt, for Joseph had the authority to protect them all.

The Jews and the first Christians recognized God's 'glory' in the whole history of the world, from the creation itself right down to their own times. Most impressive of all, for the Jews, was the escape from Egypt and the covenant God had made with them at Mount Sinai. For Christians, the life, death and resurrection of Jesus is the key to God's glory, for they show the invincible power of God's love. Here indeed is power, authority, and weight. The love which sustained the universe is released into the world, and made available, in an entirely new way. God's glory has been revealed in Jesus as never before in the world's history.

This is the source of Christian security. The promises of salvation are backed by events which make them utterly dependable. The credit worthiness of God has been established beyond any possible doubting by his Son, Jesus Christ. All the partial and inadequate glimpses of God's power in the past, all the limited explanations of his plans, fade into insignificance once Jesus is recognized.

In Jesus, the unlimited possibilities of God's love and man's response are revealed to the world. Through Jesus, all people can come to the perfection of love for which God has made them. This is how God has finally made his glory known.

PAUL'S LETTER TO THE ROMANS:
AN APPROACH THROUGH LITERATURE

by Joseph Griffiths

Even a casual reader of the letter to the Romans is impressed by the magnificence of the work. The sweep and scope of Paul's argument are breathtaking, the power of his rhetoric impressive, and yet one is continually aware of its firm construction, of the fact that he is developing an argument patiently, carefully and in a logical, orderly manner. We admire the sharpness of the intellect, and the keenness of the sensibility. Clearly, it is a letter into which much time, thought and effort has been put.

Yet Paul himself would have been horrified if his readers' admiration had not extended further than the formal and aesthetic level. He forms and shapes it so splendidly in order to convince his readers of the important truths which he intends them to grasp. They are truths which have transformed his own life, truths which he hopes will transform the lives of anyone whose heart is open to them.

The Good News is not of the same kind as that which provides a reassuring newspaper headline. We are meant to ponder its significance for our own lives, and, just as important, to let it alter us as human beings, by allowing it to influence our thoughts, words and actions. We must become new persons if we acknowledge that Paul is speaking the truth.

> 'Act from thought should quickly follow.
> What is thinking for?'

W. H. Auden's laconic advice to the sulky lover in his poem brings me to the point of these comments: namely, the way in which the readers of the letter to the Romans may be helped to understand and to apply its truth to their own lives, by considering it in conjunction with some non-biblical literature.

It is possible to agree with Paul's basic message that

'. . . the gospel reveals how God puts men right with himself: it is through faith from beginning to end.' (Romans 1:17)

Yet readers also know that bearing witness to this faith in their lives can be an arduous task. Immediately they begin to examine its consequences in living the difficulties arise. In chapter 14 Paul himself offers guidance to his Roman readers on some of the practical problems. This is helpful, but their problems are not necessarily our problems and we are still left with a formidable task.

It is my belief that literature can help us here, in a variety of ways. In the imaginative vision of life which a writer projects we can locate some of the themes with which Paul is concerned, and see how such themes work themselves out in concrete human situations as depicted by the writer. We can feel them proved on our pulses, by the emotional force with which the writer presents them.

This is not to treat other works as mere reinforcements of Pauline ideas, as the writer's views are usually quite different from Paul's. On the contrary, we can begin to appreciate the complexity of what the truth may be in the writer's rendering of life, and in real life itself, since literature is to some extent a reflection of life. For example, the reader of Shakespeare's *The Merchant of Venice* (one of the suggested works for consideration) would be rash to conclude that Shakespeare is inviting us to admire the Christian love of the Venetians, and to revile the Jewish legality of Shylock. The truth is rarely so easy. But Paul's ideas on love and law may be deepened in the reader's mind, by considering the relevance of the play to them. Unless they are questioned, they will never be held by anyone beyond the most superficial level. Life itself provides the most searching questioning of them, but literature can often be the best intermediary.

There is another way in which our reading of novels and plays can help us. Paul's letters were written for identifiable purposes, in a definite historical context. Yet he did not feel himself constricted by such considerations, as he himself tells us:

'For I have an obligation to all peoples, to the civilized and to the savage, to the educated and to the ignorant. So then, I am eager to preach the Good News to you also who live in Rome.'

Part of his obligation is to posterity, to us, whose
world is a different one from that of the Romans. It helps
us to appreciate him better if we can locate his themes in
eras nearer our own, and see how they express themselves in contexts that are more familiar to us. Literature is again of service here, for it is an imaginative
record of man's experience in time, a re-creation of
human feeling, thought and experience. Literature of our
own century has a particular relevance for us, and it is
because of this that the works selected are mainly modern
ones.

Before going on to list and discuss the selected reading,
a few cautionary remarks need to be added. There is
always the tendency when we read a novel or play to see
in it our own preoccupations, and perhaps even to dis-
tort it to do so. Critics of *Hamlet* are inclined to reveal
more about themselves than about the central character.
This tendency is especially strong if we read the work in
association with another group of ideas which we are
trying to assimilate. Therefore, we must be careful not to
import the themes of Paul's letter into our reading. We
must respect the integrity of any writer's work, just as
much as we do that of Paul himself. If we don't, then we
delude ourselves, and the literature becomes merely a
part of our delusion.

In addition, it is necessary to bear in mind that any
writer (Paul included) is working in a historical situation,
often with literary conventions in mind, and aiming at a
certain kind of audience. Shakespeare's plays were
written for an Elizabethan audience which was familiar
with his conventions, whereas a modern novelist writes
for a very different kind of reader with a different knowledge of life, who expects the author to keep to certain
conventions about novel writing. Again, we must be careful not to extract single ideas and oversimplify them,
merely because we can see a connection between them
and Paul's.

Bearing in mind the above comments, I suggest that
the following may be a convenient method of approach
to both the letter to the Romans and the suggested
literature. Read in full both the letter and the commentary. Then put both aside, and approach the literature with an open mind, allowing it to make its own

impact. Finally, return to the literature with Paul's ideas in mind, and try to see what links there are. This is the point at which the method of inquiry ought to begin to be fruitful.

Below is a list of the recommended reading:

The Merchant of Venice: William Shakespeare. An edition with introduction and notes is useful, such as the Arden or Signet editions.
The Grapes of Wrath: John Steinbeck (Penguin)
The Power and the Glory: Graham Greene (Penguin)
Waiting for Godot: Samuel Beckett (Faber)

In suggesting some lines of approach to these works and their thematic and incidental relationships with the letter to the Romans, I have tried to keep in mind its division into seven parts as outlined in the general introduction to the commentary. However, it is not wise to adhere too rigidly to this, for none of the books can be simply equated with one section, since their themes and situations are applicable to the letter at a variety of points.

It need hardly be added that my comments are tentative and incomplete, rather than exhaustive (and perhaps exhausting). The reader's reward and enjoyment will come primarily from his own perceptions and explorations.

1. Opening Remarks 1:1-17
2. Universal Guilt and Need 1:18-3:20

The two sections are merged, since they are complementary. Paul rejoices in those who have received the Good News, and is saddened by the plight of those who were unable, or are unwilling to listen to it. He has in mind both pagans and Jews.

Even though they believe in a God, their belief cannot free them from the power of sin. Their position is neither as desperate, nor as tragic as that of many modern men who cannot accept the Good News. *Waiting for Godot* is a play which depicts such a plight. Estragon and Vladimir, two tramps, wait on a country road for the arrival of Godot, a character who, they believe, will give meaning and purpose to their lives. But he never arrives, and they are left to their own devices, to their own tragi-comic antics. It is a play, and the full extent of the pathos and the comedy comes out only in performance. They don't even know who Godot is, claiming at most that 'he's a kind of acquaintance', but admitting that they 'hardly know him'. They are torn between ignoring his existence and possible arrival, and living in the hope and belief that he will come to transform their nihilistic state.

The play is full of comparisons to Christ and other figures from the New and Old Testaments. The tramps 'remember the gospels', argue about the evangelists' different versions of the salvation of the thieves crucified with Christ, and squabble when Estragon compares him-self directly with Christ. Vladimir replies:

'Christ! What's Christ got to do with it? You're not going to compare yourself to Christ?'

Clearly, Christ is not Godot, and is of little use to them in making sense of their lives. They know more than the obvious things about him, but see only a faint relevance of his position to theirs. He is no saviour for them, and they frequently express their need of being saved.

What do they stand for? Who is Godot? Answers to these questions are almost as varied as the members of any audience watching it. My own view is that Godot is that presence of God which man cannot know fully, and yet which he feels vital to his existence. The tramps appear to be modern men who know of the Christian faith, whose lives have been influenced by it, whose hopes and aspirations have been roused by it. Despite this they cannot see its significance, and they are left in the deeply tragic position of needing this God, in whom they can never wholeheartedly believe. In a later play of Beckett, *End-Game*, one character declares about God:

'The dirty dog, he doesn't even exist!'

He ought to, but there is anger because he doesn't show himself. Readers of the letter to the Romans might well begin to sense the universality and complexity of the guilt and need, which Paul depicts in the world known to him. Modern man knows of Christianity and its Good News, but finds himself unconvinced by it.

One other relationship in *Waiting for Godot* needs comment: that between Lucky and Pozzo, slave and master. This brings to mind Paul's comments in 6:15-23, where he contrasts the slaves of sin with slaves of righteousness. Pozzo quickly forgets Godot's name, and considers any encounter with him only in the most condescending terms. Pozzo is a slave to his own desires, Lucky the means by which he may fulfil them. Taken together they present man not only without God, but without even the wish for anything other than blind servitude and selfish gratification of one's own desires.

The gist of Lucky's long outburst is that no matter what physical and intellectual discoveries man makes, he is still a creature whose destiny is death. Their final exit is preceded by Pozzo's frantic despair, and his use of a horrific image for human existence, which Vladimir subsequently embroiders:

'They give birth astride of a grave, the light gleams an instant, then it's night once more.'

Their servile plight is truly horrifying. Beckett may intend them to represent the nadir of modern man's life, Vladimir and Estragon the norm or even the zenith. Beckett's vision of human life might be said to be confined to the second main section of Paul's letter; but it is a truthful, honest and deeply felt presentation of the modern world as he sees it.

3. God's Act of Salvation 3:21–5:11
5. God's Plan: Jews and Gentiles 9–11

In the first of these two sections Paul shows us that Christ is the human embodiment of God's creative love. He is the means by which atonement is made for man's guilt in a legalistic sense, by which man is freed from the slavery of sin. It is by his sacrifice that man's salvation becomes possible. Then in the second of the sections he considers the position of the Jews, who have rejected Christ and followed their own system of law, given to them by God.

The suggestion that *The Merchant of Venice* is concerned with issues as weighty as these may come as a surprise to those readers who remember the play from their school-days. Probably they will recall it as a piece of romantic fantasy concerned with strange bonds, extravagant gestures, whirlwind romances, secrets locked in caskets, and everything ending in idyllic happiness.

We have moved from the darkness of Beckett and man without Christ, to the gaiety of a Shakespearean comedy

and a Venice in which Christianity is the religion of
nearly everyone.

This is as it ought to be in the world after Christ has
entered it, the world which Paul passionately wishes to
come about, the world which we might like to associate
with our childhood innocence. But Paul and Shakespeare and we know that this is not the whole truth. For
Paul there are the Jews, for Shakespeare Shylock, and
from my own childhood I recall a fierce, proud Shylock,
played by Donald Wolfit, threatening to break the
fragility of the fairy tale.

As soon as the reader returns to the play he will sense
the force and power that emanate from Shylock, and
begin to realize that either he is out of place in the
romantic world of the play, or, more likely, the play is
more complicated than he remembered. The romance,
gaiety and joy are still there, but we see them in a different perspective, when we consider Shylock's significance.
He lives by the law, enters into a barbarous bond, and
demands his full contractual dues by it:

'My deeds upon my head! I crave the law,
The penalty and forfeit of my bond.'

This is his rejection of Portia's famous plea for mercy on
Antonio's behalf.

He lives by law, not by love. Yet even this is not accur-
ate. He goes 'in hate' to the Christians, hates Antonio
'for he is a Christian', bears grudges, and savours his
revenge. Shylock's references to 'holy Abram', 'father
Abram' recall Paul's words in Romans 4:16:

'The promise was based on faith, then, in order that the
promise should be guaranteed as God's free gift to all
of Abraham's descendants – not just those who obey
the Law, but also those who believe as Abraham did.
For Abraham is the spiritual father of us all.'

Shylock stands condemned even by Judaic standards.

It would be reassuring if we could turn to the Christians
in the play, to find that they are the embodiment of
Christian faith and love. To some extent we do. Antonio
is prepared to sacrifice his wealth and his life for Bassanio.
Launcelot quotes an Elizabethan proverb (based upon
2 Corinthians 12:9) when he quits the servitude of
Shylock's house for service to Bassanio:

'The old proverb is very well parted between my master
Shylock and you, sir: you have the grace of God, sir,
and he hath enough.'

The Duke himself urges Shylock to 'gentleness and love'.

However, there is another side to the picture. Few
modern readers can go through the play without feeling
sympathy for, and indignation on behalf of, Shylock,
whatever the scholars may tell us about Elizabethan
attitudes to Jews (and we might remember that Shakespeare was no ordinary Elizabethan).

The Christians treat him abominably. Antonio agrees
with Shylock that he is just as likely to go on reviling him
as he has done in the past. Lorenzo robs him with
Jessica's aid. Children mock him in the streets after he is
robbed. Gratiano rails at him throughout the trial scene,
gloating over his humiliation. His obligatory conversion
to Christianity is perhaps the unkindest cut of all.

Paul's warning to the Christians at 11:26 against
complacence, 'thinking how wise you are', needs to be
heeded by many of the Christians in *The Merchant of
Venice*. Shylock's impassioned self-justification at III.i.
47ff points out the faults of the Christians, and is left
unanswered:

'If a Jew wrong a Christian, what is his humility?
Revenge. If a Christian wrong a Jew, what should his
sufferance be by Christian example? Why, revenge.
The villainy you teach me I will execute . . .'

Merely listening to the Good News and accepting it
nominally leaves men no better off than those who reject
it altogether. We must also allow the Holy Spirit to pour
'his love into our hearts' (Romans 5:5).

So far the main principle of this love in the play has
been touched upon only incidentally. Undoubtedly it is
to be found in Belmont and with Portia.

It is easy to appreciate Portia's role as the exponent of
love and mercy in the trial scene, but in the caskets
scenes this is not quite so obvious. There is a fairy-tale
quality in these scenes which is delightful, but, as in
many fairy tales, the underlying issues are serious ones,
which are related in theme and language to what is
happening in Venice.

How this is so can best be understood by considering
the caskets and their scrolls:

'This first, of gold, who this inscription bears:
"Who chooseth me shall gain what many men desire."
The second, silver, which this promise carries:
"Who chooseth me shall get as much as he deserves."
This third, dull lead, with warning all as blunt:
"Who chooseth me must give and hazard all he hath." ' '

Words such as 'gain', 'deserves' and 'hazard' all remind us
of the commercial transactions of Venice, of the world of
profit and loss, of the selfishness that arises therefrom.

When we consider the meaning of the riddles on the
scrolls in their context, we begin to realize that those who
choose gold and silver seek to fulfil their own desires, to
demand their rights and dues because of their own efforts.
In Paul's words, they 'boast before God' (Romans 4:2),
unlike Abraham, who simply puts his trust and faith in
God, and is thereby pleasing to him. The man who
chooses the leaden casket trustingly gives himself. This is
very close to what Paul is trying to express about man's
relationship with God, when he discusses Abraham:

'God promised Abraham and his descendants that the
world would belong to him. This promise was made,
not because Abraham obeyed the Law, but because he
believed and was accepted as righteous by God.'
(Romans 4:13)

Portia's father was no whimsical, old eccentric, but a man
who understood the spirit in which life ought to be lived.

The world of Belmont typifies this generous, trusting
spirit, which leads men to give themselves freely to one
another. After Bassanio has chosen correctly, Portia
dedicates her life to him in the same spirit with which
Paul urges his Roman readers to dedicate theirs to God:

'Happiest of all is that her gentle spirit
Commits itself to yours to be directed,
As from her lord, her governor, her king.'

4. God's Power Overcomes Human Weakness 5:12-8:39

This central section of the letter is the core of what Paul
is trying to communicate. In a variety of ways he tries to
show us how God's creative love for man expresses itself
through Jesus, conquering sin and death, and through
the Holy Spirit, continuing to resist the imperfections of
human nature in order to give us life in the Father.

A novel which gives us the opportunity of reflecting

upon these ideas and seeing them at work in a world
closer to our own is *The Power and the Glory*. In a long
BBC interview Greene said that he felt that it was his best
novel. He also recounted the story of his interview with
Pope Paul, in which he told us that his novel enjoyed the
distinction of being condemned by the Holy Office but
read and admired by Pope Paul himself. I think the other
Paul would have enjoyed it if he were still with us!

Greene's view of the natural and human world, like
Beckett's, is depressing. The opening pages depict an
arid, dusty Mexican town, where vultures perch lazily on
the roof, sharks coast in the near-by bay, Mr Tench keeps
his nausea under control by spitting and is roused by the
sound of a revolver holster creaking. Man is either
carrion or killer. This sense of desolation is deepened as
we proceed, until Luis's father sums it all up, when he tells
his son that 'We have been deserted.'

Ironically, it is the Lieutenant who epitomizes the
emptiness of this world. He badly wants to reform the
corrupt society around him, to run an honest and
efficient administration, to give to the poor some of the
necessary material benefits of the world, and to use his
'power' to good purpose.

Greene compares the Lieutenant's austerity and sense
of dedication to that of a monk. But he hates pleasure
and cannot even enjoy a simple game of cards. Moreover,
he has little that is positive to live for. The 'truth' to be
conveyed to children is that of

'. . . a vacant universe and a cooling world, the right
to be happy in any way they choose.'

Yet when he looks at the children he

'. . . became aware in his own heart of a sad and un-
satisfiable love.'

In contrast to Beckett, Greene does not leave us at the
level of a meaningless existence.

When we turn to the Priest, we discern the struggle for
something positive. We might notice here that neither
the Priest, nor the Lieutenant is named. They are meant
to be representative, even allegorical figures. The Priest
typifies the struggle described so movingly and so
vividly by Paul in Romans 7:14-25:

'So I find that this law is at work: when I want to do
what is good, what is evil is the only choice I have. My

inner being delights in the law of God. But I see a
different law at work in my body . . .'
When the Priest is on the run, and the villagers are
hesitant about sheltering him, he snaps angrily at them:
'It's not what you want or what I want.'

He has led a sinful life, epitomized by his illegitimate
child, Brigitta. It is ironic that it is she who helps to
awaken the spirit of love in him. His reactions to her
contrast markedly with those of the Lieutenant to
children. His heart jumps at her name, 'with its secret
and appalling love'. He is aware of the 'Power' that
expresses itself in creation.

The novel traces the course of the Priest's responses to
this love, and the reader will follow them for himself, and
make his own judgements on the nature of the Priest's
development. But it may help to draw attention to the
conversation between the two men after the Priest's
capture, when they discuss the love of God. The Lieutenant mocks the Priest's platitudes about 'God is Love',
and about God's justice. The Priest replies heatedly and
earnestly:

'. . . God *is* love. I don't say the heart doesn't feel a
taste of it, but what a taste, the smallest glass of love
mixed with a pint pot of ditch-water. We wouldn't
recognize *that* love. It might even look like hate. It
would be enough to scare us – God's love.'
He is so terrified at the power of God's love that he
finally declares, 'I just want justice, that's all.'

The force of love which sends Christ into the world is
one which amazes Paul and terrifies the Priest. Even in
the Lieutenant it finally provokes 'bitter kindness' to the
Priest, as he tells him to sleep.

The conclusion to the novel hints at the Priest's salvation, but the reader is left to decide the issue. However,
we remember that the Priest returns with the Judas
figure, the mestizzo from the physical security and comfort of the Lehrs, in answer to the criminal's ambiguous
message, 'For Christ's sake, father . . .'

The hint becomes still stronger on the final pages, when
Luis spits at the Lieutenant in scorn, and kneels to kiss
the new priest's hand in welcome. The spirit of the Priest
is still at work, indicative of the other Spirit whom Paul
writes about.

The feeling behind the novel is very much that which Paul expresses at Romans 11:33:

'How great are God's riches! How deep are his wisdom and knowledge! Who can explain his decisions? Who can understand his ways?'

The Priest is influenced by the power of love to acquire some of this wisdom, when in the prison cell he speaks tenderly and with pity to that most unlovable of creatures, the pious, sanctimonious woman, as she threatens to report him to the bishop, who has escaped to security across the border:

'When you visualized a man or woman carefully, you could always begin to feel pity . . . that was a quality God's image carried with it . . .'

6. Practical Advice for Life in Christ 12:1-15:13
7. Plans, Greetings and Conclusion 15:14-16:27

In the first of these sections Paul brings us firmly down to earth, as he describes the way men behave to one another in a Christ-like way, the way in which such relationships form 'the body of Christ'. The final section shows this happening among people that are known to him.

Although I have chosen *The Grapes of Wrath* as being particularly appropriate to this section, any of the previous works might prompt reflections upon it. For all the despair evident in *Waiting for Godot*, the tramps stay together and show concern for one another. One suggestion is that they are meant to be seen as different parts of one personality. The whisky Priest in *The Power and the Glory* is a model of Christ-like behaviour (as outlined by Paul in chapter 14), in his efforts to serve those whom he meets. Almost everyone he meets is touched by his spirit (in many senses), and benefits from the encounter. In *The Merchant of Venice*, Shakespeare attempts the well-nigh impossible task of reconciling the worlds of Belmont and Venice in the bargain of faith and the usury of love.

When we consider the above works, we can realize the diversity and complexity of the way in which men behave to one another. In addition, we can see that they develop and change. 'The body of Christ' should not be dissected on the cold slab of doctrinal theology, because it is a dynamic body, exercising itself in the world of men.

The Grapes of Wrath gives us an opportunity to consider part of the complex social body of the USA as the economic stresses compel change, and force the 'Okies' westward from their homes to the promised land of California. Their native community is in decay, and they are forced to find new work, new roles, a new life.

Jim Casy (perhaps his initials are meant to be suggestive), a formerly hypocritical preacher, tries to make some real discoveries about people, instead of simply preying upon them:

'I ain't gonna baptize. I'm gonna work in the fiel's, in the green fiel's, an' I'm gonna be near to folks. I ain't gonna try to teach 'em nothin'. I'm gonna try to learn.'

When he re-enters the novel near the end, he is leading the strikers in their fight for justice, using his strength in their cause, and is murdered because of his involvement.

Casy proves the inspiration to Tom Joad, the central character, who enters the novel as a murderer returning from prison. In trouble because he attacked Casy's killer, Tom is sheltered by Ma. He tells her of his belief in Casy's ideals, which he repeats:

'Says one time he went out in the wilderness to find his own soul, an' he foun' he didn' have no soul that was his'n. Says he foun' he just got a little piece of a great big soul.'

Earlier in chapter 18, Ma expresses similar sentiments to Rose of Sharon, who is pregnant, when they are both saddened by the impending death of Granma. The family is a body, and Steinbeck registers its life and vigour. But we see how the impersonal forces of a modern economic system imperil it, and threaten destruction. Yet the sense of family and community extends to other families in need, the Wilsons. It is not an exclusive thing. Nor is the spirit it engenders completely destroyed.

In the final scene of the novel Rose of Sharon feeds the starving man from her own body, with the milk from her breasts. It is not the milk which they could have foreseen flowing in the promised land. But it is the milk of human kindness, ennobling and nurturing mankind. The echo of Christ's giving of his own body to man to eat is inescapable. The same idea is suggested earlier in the Highway 66 café. The hardbitten Al growls at Mae when she refuses the poor family cheap bread:

'God Almighty, Mae, give 'em bread.'
Even the mercenary Mae sells the children candy cheaply.

Steinbeck's sense of the closeness of men's connection with one another is evident throughout the novel. However, he is scornful of attempting to coerce men into a fearful or unwilling conformity. The reassuring harmony of the migrants in the government camp is threatened more by the so-called Jesus-lover, the 'brown woman', than by the enemies from without. She is too arrogant to consider that Jesus might be able to help her, but tries to intimidate Rose of Sharon into decorous behaviour by invoking the idea of a God ever ready to catch man out:

'I'm a-helpin' Jesus watch the goin's on. An' you an' them other sinners ain't gittin' away with it.'

She is far from the Christian fellowship achieved by Rose of Sharon herself. Her association with Christ by the use of his name only serves to emphasize how remote she is from that true acceptance of one another in Christ, stated so simply and aptly by Paul in the letter:

'Accept one another, then, for the glory of God, as Christ has accepted you.' Romans 15:7

THE BIBLE READING FELLOWSHIP

Readers of this commentary may wish to follow a regular pattern of Bible reading, designed to cover the Bible roughly on the basis of a book a month. Suitable Notes (send for details) with helpful exposition and prayers are provided by the Bible Reading Fellowship three times a year (January to April, May to August, September to December), and are available from:—

UK   The Bible Reading Fellowship,
            St Michael's House,
            2 Elizabeth Street,
            London, SW1W 9RQ

USA   The Bible Reading Fellowship,
            P.O. Box 299, Winter Park,
            Florida 32789, USA.

AUSTRALIA   The Bible Reading Fellowship,
            Jamieson House,
            Constitution Avenue, Reid,
            Canberra, ACT 2601,
            Australia.

Also available in the Fontana Religious Series

What is Real in Christianity?
DAVID L. EDWARDS

The author strips away the legends from Jesus to show the man who is real, relevant and still fascinating. A clear, confident statement of Christian faith taking account of all criticisms.

Parents, Children and God
ANTHONY BULLEN

This book attempts to guide parents in their role as Christian educators. How they may answer their children's questions, how they may meet their children's needs from infancy to adolescence, how they may pray with their children, how they may talk to their children about sex: these and other topics are dealt with.

Ethics in a Permissive Society
WILLIAM BARCLAY

Professor Barclay approaches difficult and vexed questions with his usual humanity and clarity, asking what Christ himself would say or do in our world today.

Dialogue with Youth
AINSLIE MEARES

'This is a first-class general introduction to the world of young adults. . . . (It) is in general terms which convey a wealth of valuable insight . . . a quantity survey which helps to identify and map out a field of personal encounter in which few are competent, many are hesitant, all are involved.'

Church Times

Also available in the Fontana Religious Series

The Divine Pity
GERALD VANN

Undoubtedly Gerald Vann's masterpiece. Many people have insisted that this book should not merely be read, but re-read constantly, for it becomes more valuable the more it is pondered upon.

The Founder of Christianity
C. H. DODD

A portrait of Jesus by the front-ranking New Testament scholar. 'A first-rate and fascinating book . . . this book is a theological event.'   *Times Literary Supplement*

Science and Christian Belief
C. A. COULSON

'Professor Coulson's book is one of the most profound studies of the relationship of science and religion that has yet been published.'   *Times Literary Supplement*

Something Beautiful for God
MALCOLM MUGGERIDGE

'For me, Mother Teresa of Calcutta embodies Christian love in action. Her face shines with the love of Christ on which her whole life is centred. *Something Beautiful for God* is about her and the religious order she has instituted.'

Malcolm Muggeridge

Jesus Rediscovered
MALCOLM MUGGERIDGE

'. . . one of the most beautifully written, perverse, infuriating, enjoyable and moving books of the year.'

David L. Edwards, Church Times

Also available in the Fontana Religious Series

Something Beautiful for God
MALCOLM MUGGERIDGE

'For me, Mother Teresa of Calcutta embodies Christian love in action. Her face shines with the love of Christ on which her whole life is centred. *Something Beautiful for God* is about her and the religious order she has instituted.'

Malcolm Muggeridge

Instrument of Thy Peace
ALAN PATON

'Worthy of a permanent place on the short shelf of enduring classics of the life of the Spirit.'

Henry P. van Dusen, Union Theological Seminary

Sing A New Song
THE PSALMS IN TODAY'S ENGLISH VERSION

These religious poems are of many kinds: there are hymns of praise and worship of God; prayers for help, protection, and salvation; pleas for forgiveness; songs of thanksgiving for God's blessings; and petitions for the punishment of enemies. This translation of the *Psalms in Today's English Version* has the same freshness and clarity of language, the same accuracy of scholarship based on the very best originals available as *Good News for Modern Man* and *The New Testament in Today's English Version.*

The Gospel According to Peanuts
ROBERT L. SHORT

This book has made a lasting appeal to people of all denominations and none. It has been read and enjoyed by literally millions of people. A wonderfully imaginative experiment in Christian communication.

Also available in the Fontana Religious Series

How Modern Should Theology Be?
HELMUT THIELICKE

'Thielicke touches on basic theological issues for today, but he does it with such a light hand, and with such graphic powers of illustration that I really cannot recall any other modern preacher who is so much *au fait* with modern theological questions.'
Ronald Gregor Smith

Strange Victory
GORDON W. IRESON

The Gospel, we are told, is Good News. What of? When we invite a man to become a Christian, what exactly are we offering to him, and asking him? These are some of the questions this book seeks to answer.

Companion to the Good News
JOSEPH RHYMER and ANTHONY BULLEN

More than 30 million people have bought *Good News for Modern Man* since it was first published. This 'Companion' has been written to help people understand the New Testament.

Apologia Pro Vita Sua
J. H. NEWMAN

A passionate defence of Cardinal Newman's own intellectual and spiritual integrity by a man who had been under continuous attack for many years.